The Thumbnail
Circumnavigation

To my family

The Thumbnail Circumnavigation

Paul Packwood

SEAFARER BOOKS

© Paul Packwood 2006

First published in the UK by
Seafarer Books
102 Redwald Road
Rendlesham
Woodbridge
Suffolk IP12 2TE
www.seafarerbooks.com

ISBN-10 0 9550243 4 X
ISBN-13 978 0 9550243 4 4

A CIP catalogue record for this book is available from the British Library

Edited by Hugh Brazier
Typesetting and design by Julie Rainford
Cover design by Louis Mackay
Photographs from the author's private collection, except where otherwise credited

Printed in Finland by WS Bookwell OY

CONTENTS

1

Introduction

Of course it is not necessary to have an excuse, a reason, or an ambition in order to go sailing. Many go sailing for the sheer pleasure of just being waterborne; they do not have to race, to explore, to be challenged, to get from point A to point B as fast as possible, to show their mastery over wind and tide, or to exercise their skills with electronic gadgetry. They are content on the day with the day, be they fair-weather sailors or those with derring-do. Some enthusiasts happily navigate the same waters countless times every season, pastures new are not for them an attraction. The motivation of sailors varies enormously.

So too does the variety of boats they are sailing. Thus there are ocean-going racing machines, family cruising yachts, racing dinghies, Old Gaffers, Thames Barges, Wherries and Cobles, surfboards and jet-skis. These days most sailing craft are made of glass fibre but there are still plenty about which are made of wood, of metal and even some of concrete.

This diversity of craft is matched only by the broad spectrum of characters who sail in them. On their decks, in their cockpits and in their cabins are their skippers and crews, maybe single-handed but more probably members of a team, be they family, friends or professionals. Some will have qualifications, more will just have experience, and some will be at the foot of the learning curve. The owners, the skippers, the helmsmen and the crews sharing the experiences of life afloat will be a motley bunch. They will come from different backgrounds with different accents, jobs, genders, ages, pocketbooks, attitudes and beliefs but on the water they are all members of one brotherhood – at least temporarily. If you point your boat in the right direction you may get a wave back from a royal or a prime minister.

Now the idea of deliberately pointing one's boat in a chosen direction brings me to the subject of this book. When I sail I do tend to do exactly that, having a place, a venue or an event in mind. Very often I don't make much progress in that chosen direction, but that's by the way. Probably my first venture along these lines was when the pirate radio ships were causing such controversy round our coasts and I spent a weekend sailing out of the Orwell in search of the *Ross Revenge*, anchored in Black Deep, where the disc jockeys of Radio Caroline were doing their thing. Later I made rendezvous with the tiny replica *Godspeed* as she proceeded down Galleons Reach in the Lower Thames at the start of her commemorative Atlantic crossing to Virginia. Then I took to exploring the inland waterways, after first of all making the necessary coastal passages to gain access to them. Using this formula I was able to probe the Rivers Lee and Stort, Old Father Thames, the Kennet & Avon Canal and the Leeds and Liverpool canal. I also circumnavigated East Anglia twice from my Ipswich base – the first time in a clockwise direction and several years later the opposite way round. More recently I was bet £100, by my sceptical son, that I could not sail my little 18-foot Seatrekker to Salcombe in Devon to see the total eclipse of 1999. I won the bet with a few hours to spare but the debt is still unpaid!

Since that exploit, in recent years, I had not accomplished

a great deal due to the pressures of life in retirement and problems with the ageing boat (boats seem to age at twice the rate of we humans and they show it unforgivingly). Thus in 2003 I had to be content with a very enjoyable cruise up the coast and across the Norfolk Broads to Norwich, while the following year I got no further than Iken on the River Alde.

This progressive scaling-down of my little trips began to worry me. The members of my family seemed to be running out of genuine reasons for preventing me from going on safari. One daughter had emigrated to Australia and the other had sold up and moved onto a narrowboat on the Lancaster canal – so neither of them now needed the biennial help decorating and licking wildernesses into shape which had become customary in recent years as they moved their university digs and then set up house. My son's house was now in immaculate decorative condition and my wife was finding it harder to invent jobs around our house and garden which really did need doing. What was more sinister were the hints that it was time for me to give up sailing. These were growing into positive assertions that I was past it, just too old, a danger to myself and other people.

When the average human being is faced with an almost incessant barrage of denigration it does inevitably have an effect, and I began to wonder if collectively they were not right. Perhaps I really ought to get rid of the boat (I doubted whether anyone would actually buy it), and content myself with the garden and maybe, for a year or two longer, the caravan. If I insisted on keeping the boat then perhaps I could be satisfied to cruise up and down the Orwell ('After all it's such a lovely river'), with an occasional cruise in company for safety's sake to the Walton Backwaters. My crafty maritime advisers and well-wishers were also not slow or unwilling to exaggerate, aggravate and exploit the problems I was having with the 40-year-old boat. The plywood relic, did, I had to admit, take an inordinate amount of time each year, scraping it, painting and varnishing it, and attacking it with saws, chisels, drills and screwdrivers. I also had to confess that I secretly marvelled each year that I did not develop pneumoconiosis from the burning-off and application of costly coats of anti-fouling.

The cumulative effect of this campaign of calculated scepticism was to encourage me to attempt an unbiased, objectively subjective, critical analysis of the whole situation. There was not a lot I could do about my age, except deny it. Yes, I did suffer a little from arthritis and stiffness and admittedly at night I sometimes got cramp, but usually in only one leg at a time. Alright my eyesight was not brilliant but I carried a good pair of binoculars on board and at sea there wasn't much to hear so I would not need both my hearing aids. The fact that I suffer from 'white finger' when the temperature falls below 30 Celsius could be ignored since my trips usually at least started in high summer. All I needed to do to continue with my boating, it seemed to me, in my constructively self-critical appraisal, was to have a sight test and possibly new spectacles, and always take with me ample supplies of ibuprofen painkillers and glucosamine tablets.

There was, however, one more and crucially important result of all this welter of well-meant but negative advice. My zest for sailing was being diminished, my confidence in my competence was being sapped, my willingness to endure the discomforts and inconveniences on board was being reduced, and I was beginning to doubt whether the rewards justified all the pre-launch inputs of effort and expense. In short, I was beginning to totter on my sea legs. But when I thought things over it struck me forcibly that giving things up prematurely, before one actually *had* to, could only be self-harming and in the end self-destructive. As a natural coward I could not bear the thought of harming myself, and the notion of suicide was even less attractive.

So, when the weather turned warmer in the spring of 2005 I commenced the annual refit – in the front garden, where *Plover* had spent the winter. There was a great deal needing to be done. Apart from the usual cosmetic work and the anti-fouling, I had in mind some alterations to stowage in the cockpit and in the cabin. Additionally the paddle-wheel speed and distance recorder had to be replaced.

I had not got very far with this programme of work when I chanced by accident on details of the Horatio Nelson/Battle of Trafalgar Bicentenary Celebrations to be held at Portsmouth at the end of June – including a Review of the Fleet by the Queen, a simulated battle and fireworks. The prospect of witnessing this historic occasion, which would obviously never be repeated in my lifetime, excited me greatly and I began to look seriously into the possibility of participating – what a great excuse for a trip!

The idea of re-visiting Portsmouth, the Isle of Wight and the Solent area was very appealing and my mind wandered erratically over possible itineraries. I have a natural antipathy to U-turns: I just resist the idea of turning round and coming back the same way – whether walking, cycling, motoring or sailing. I always prefer a round trip. So I began to consider, from a very early stage, what should be my route back home after the naval celebrations? To circumnavigate the Isle of Wight and head back home using different ports and anchorages would be an easy option. But what about hopping over to France, either from Pompey or from Yarmouth, IoW? I would just love to do this, but the trouble was the cross-channel distance coupled with the complication of sailing at right angles across two very busy shipping lanes. As a single-hander I would find it difficult to maintain a proper watch 'at all times', as required by the International Regulations and common sense. As a *senior* solo sailor with a tendency to nod off at the slightest opportunity, unless stimulated by absolutely riveting TV, a pair of pretty legs, food or a hovercraft less than a cable away, I had to admit that I would find it quite impossible to keep a proper watch.

This left the option of carrying on westward as far as possible and for as long as time would permit. If I got as far as Salcombe again I would be satisfied, anywhere beyond that, very pleased. I scarcely dared to dream about the ultimate fulfilment of a long-standing dream – to round Land's End and sail up the Bristol Channel to Avonmouth, returning across country through the inland waterways.

The result of all this dreaming and cogitation was that, yes, I would get the boat into the water as soon as I possibly could and hopefully in time to try to get to Portsmouth. From there I would do whatever seemed possible. My zest for the boating life now rekindled, I set to work with a will – playing table tennis a little less frequently, cutting down the lawn-mowing to once a week, ignoring the existence of the pressure washer, delegating the cleaning of the car to my wife and deferring the redecoration of the larger back bedroom until the autumn.

By dint of all this careful management and after a really skimpy refit, doing only what was absolutely vital and minimising the cosmetic work, *Plover* was launched uncommonly early in the season at the end of May. During the second weekend of June I took her downriver on a proving trial. Most of the Saturday was spent loading and stowing gear and checking apparatus and systems, so it was early evening before we finally got away from the yacht club pontoon. We anchored for the night off Trimley when rain began to fall. Next morning we continued down to

Harwich and then up the Stour to Holbrook Creek, returning to Ipswich on Sunday. The twenty-four hours or so spent on board did serve a variety of useful purposes, important among which were to confirm that the hull was not leaking, that the outboard motor was in good fettle and that the sails and rigging were all A1.

But probably the most important proving of the trial was that of myself. Was I still able and willing to submit to the strictures and constrictions of life aboard a small boat for any length of time. In this respect it was a very good trial. This early in the season the boat was a long way from being well organised so aggravations were at a peak. As a cruise develops one becomes better organised and life becomes more bearable, perhaps even agreeable. It all depends upon arrangements down below – the layout of the cabin is crucial.

On *Plover* the open cockpit and cabin take up roughly equal sections of the boat. The cabin is really a floating storeroom – for food and drink, for fresh water, for life jackets, for sails, for books, charts and flares, for clothing, for bedding and a host of miscellaneous boating bric-a-brac. Every nook and cranny, above the floorboards and below, is stuffed full, and to find anything almost inevitably involves moving half-a-dozen other things first – rather like in one of those flat puzzles you find in Christmas crackers. Cooking is by Camping Gaz on two burners and an inefficient grill. The galley work surface doubles as a chart table when under way. There is a small sink under the stove but no toilet on board and this does somewhat restrict the range of permitted natural functions. There is sitting headroom only in the cabin, which serves, therefore, mostly as a place only for eating and sleeping, neither activity with a high degree of comfort.

At the end of the cruising day it is my custom to wriggle into the cabin, move some of the pieces of the puzzle about until the stove becomes visible and then open one or two tins. As there is no place to relax or sit comfortably I then usually unroll my sleeping bag and turn in, listening to the radio until I fall asleep. Sleeping is not normally a great problem, one is normally so tired that the hardness and narrowness of the bunk goes unnoticed, and it is really no great hardship having to pick one's pillow off the floor every few hours.

As we headed back up the Orwell at the conclusion of the brief proving trial I thought of all of these details and inevitably thought of the currently popular 'Get me out of here ...' TV programmes. I asked myself, Was I really up for this maritime version of self-inflicted hardship? Was I still willing to go? After some moments of doubt I thought of the trials and tribulations of Lord Horatio and his men, and shamefacedly decided forthwith that I had better join Her Majesty in paying due and proper tribute.

2

The cruise begins

It was a mere two weeks after the proving trial that I actually set off for Portsmouth. These were two frantic weeks devoted primarily to leaving the house and garden and our affairs generally in reasonably shipshape order and therefore leaving the boat still in very much end-of-season condition. Finally at 1745 on Sunday 19 June 2005 I cast off from the Orwell Yacht Club pontoon and motored slowly out of Fox's channel into the River Orwell. Conrad, my son, took some photos while Margot, my wife, waved unconvincingly with her hand while shaking her head in dubious and disapproving disbelief.

The trip downriver went well. The weather was fine, the tide in mild opposition. I had thought simply to get down to Trimley Marshes this first day, mooring up there for the night to give me time to complete the stowage and organisation of the boat. However, as we reached there in only an hour and a half, this seemed to be the waste of an evening so we continued on to Shotley, past the huge container ship tied up at the Trinity Wharf, Felixstowe, across the Stour confluence, past Harwich and out beyond the Dovercourt breakwater into Pennyhole Bay.

At half past nine in the evening we smugly dropped anchor in Walton Backwaters at the back of Stone Point, having made a satisfactory start. As planned, a heavenly full moon shone benignly down across the glassy water towards *Plover*.

I find that as soon as one gets afloat one's behaviour pattern changes. It's as though the first movement of the boat is like clicking a default key on a computer – one previously selected set of commands is immediately superseded by another, including the hour of reveille. So it was that as soon as it got light I woke up and immediately felt ready for action, all traces of drowsiness gone in a flash. After a cup of tea and the weather forecast I started the engine and we got under way at 0620 on a calm, misty and warm morning. Our bows were among the first of the day to disturb the peaceful surface of the Backwaters. We gently slid round the little buoys of Stone Point and into Pennyhole Bay, where we contoured round the Pye Sand and headed for the Naze.

There was no point in trying to use the sails, there was not a breath of wind. After an hour and a quarter we had Walton pier a cable to starboard, after which we very gradually drew away from the shoreline. Apart from one fishing boat off the Naze there were no craft anywhere and only lobster pots to worry about. Breakfast on the move seemed not only sensible and desirable but downright gloriously delightful. This was what I had been dreaming about for weeks and I revelled in the fact that we were at last truly on our way, and in near-perfect conditions. The sea was calm, the air was soft and warm. But it was quite misty. In fact there was no horizon ahead.

With breakfast over and Clacton pier abeam I checked the bilges and got my first surprise of the trip. When I lifted the first of the floorboards I was amazed to discover a dense mass of foam – there were bubbles everywhere. They seemed to pose no threat and after a little rummaging I traced the cause to a bottle of detergent which had become upset and had mixed with a bilge half full of water. I tasted this apprehensively. Happily it was not salty and I concluded that it must be drinking water from the flexible tank under the bunk in the bows of the boat – this must have been overfilled at the club pontoon. We continued cleanly on our way into the persisting mist. Overhead a hazy sun was trying to break through; all around the surface of the sea was scarcely disturbed.

As we turned away from the Essex coast and headed through the Wallet Spitway towards Kent, problems arose with my basic navigating equipment. The Tillerpilot, an automatic steering device, refused to hold a course and incredibly for a time the compass had a spasm of epileptic fits. The card swung wildly this way and that with no apparent cause. I did the obvious, checking that I had not moved anything magnetic near to it and that nothing in the bilges had fallen within a metre or so, but that was not the case and it remained a mystery. Happily after a while it seemed to solve itself.

Our course had become erratic so when we sighted buoys as we crossed the Barrow and Black Deeps of the Thames Estuary we went over to them to get a positive fix. The continuing poor visibility and the increased strength of the ebbing tide compounded the problems of navigation. These were further aggravated by the fact that the echo sounder was 'on the blink' while, down below, the paddle-wheel log was obviously not recording distance as it should. I was thankful that the weather was mercifully kind.

Without too much anxiety we found our way to the Shingles. From there I had two course options – either the South or the North Edinburgh channel. The southernmost was the shorter but also the shallower of the two, and it was also unbuoyed. Visibility was now really not very good and the tide was ebbing fairly vigorously. Nevertheless we gave this route preference, mainly in order to avoid being run down by the commercial shipping which uses the buoyed northern channel. I did not feel that I could trust the autopilot, and the readings of the electronic Bidata – as regards depth, speed and distance – were either suspect or just not there. When, therefore, the compass threw another fit I decided, uncharacteristically, to turn back and take the North Edinburgh Channel. We struggled back to the Shingles Patch, where I took stock of the situation. There I reasoned that it seemed sensible to let the tide have its way while we had a breather and some food and tried to sort out some of our problems. Accordingly we dropped anchor for a couple of hours.

Before getting under way again I removed the compass from its bracket and checked it out but could find nothing wrong. I also confirmed our position with my old Magellan GPS handset. With improved visibility and the ebb tide much reduced, we again set off down the southern channel. After a short while a large sandbank appeared on the bow, with a score of seals sunning themselves all over it, and it was clear that we were through the channel and had arrived off the Tongue Sand. This we now skirted discreetly, cursing the default of the echo sounder. Then, using the sun as a check on the compass, we steered for the Kent coast for an anchorage for the night.

When the twin towers of Reculver appeared out of the haze my first thoughts were to make for Whitstable, but the continuing ebb would have made that a slow and boring grind and a rather pointless one at that, since it would simply have meant retracing our course along the coast next day. A better plan, in the calm and hopefully settled conditions prevailing, would be to anchor off the Kent coast for the night. This should present no problems, providing the anchor did not drag.

Again regretting the absence of an echo bounced from the seabed, we dropped the hook at 1840. I checked the masthead light, which was OK, and the bilges, where I found more fresh water.

I now became consciously hungry and found some chilli con carne to heat up with a tin of marrowfat peas. To complete my main course I mixed a half cup of water with some potato mash powder – and opened a bottle of red wine. My delicious fifteen-minute evening meal was then rounded off with a fruit pie and tinned custard. Before drifting off into contented slumber I just had time to take a quinine tablet to minimise the possibility of an attack of cramp in the confined spaces of my narrow bunk and cramped cabin.

With the alarm on my mobile phone set for 0530 I caught the early-morning shipping forecast, which suggested that we should be able, without too much difficulty, to get round the North Foreland and into the Straits of Dover. Winds would be mostly westerly force 3–4 and diminishing.

My first job of the day was to top up the fuel tanks, and this I did not wisely but too well. Unfortunately I overfilled the port tank and about half a litre of petrol dribbled down into the bilges. I sponged this out as best I could, raised all the floorboards, left them up and paid the penalty of going without tea and toast for my breakfast.

At 0900 I raised the anchor and set off along the Kent coast in conditions of an overcast but warm, flat calm. After about an hour a slight breeze led me to unfurl the jib and, not long after that, the mainsail. By noon we had cruised gently past Margate and were rounding the North Foreland in calm conditions. Shortly afterwards we lost the tide but continued under full sail to Ramsgate where, after clearing the buoyed entrance channel we hove-to for a cheese and pickle lunch. During the lunch break *Plover* drifted a mile or so offshore and about half a mile back towards the buoyed channel.

The light breeze had freshened a little so, forgetting about the outboard, we set off under full sail across Sandwich Bay, sailing for the sheer pleasure of it and ignoring the South Foreland – the next headland we had to get round. In the euphoria of silent sunshine combined with a contented stomach I found myself unable to fight off a succession of fleeting catnaps. Fortunately we had the bay to ourselves.

Our course took us to a point about a couple of miles north of Deal, where I furled the sails and started the engine. We motored along the coast past Deal, with its pier jutting out into the shallow water. Approaching the South Foreland the sky progressively darkened, the wind increased to force 3 and the calm surface became ruffled. A thunderstorm seemed likely so I got my heavy-weather gear on. Unnecessarily so, for the threat was an idle one and calm returned, though accompanied by the poor visibility of misty conditions. We rounded the South Foreland at 1700 and steered offshore to give a reasonable clearance to the busy entrances to Dover.

Cruising past this busy ferry port can be tricky enough even in clear weather, such is the volume of traffic. Larger yachts fit radar reflectors, which give them a visible blip on the screens of other pleasure and commercial craft. *Plover* had no radar reflector to emphasise our miniscule presence. In poor visibility I just had to judge the arrival times and collision courses of ferries and other craft that I could see or hear. With conventional ferry boats steaming at 20 knots or so and hovercraft and catamarans roaring at you at nearly twice that speed, crossing their tracks is a fairly hairy business. The jet-powered vessels come thundering out of the mist at short range minutes after your ears have picked up their threatened approach. As we approached the eastern entrance we gave way to a Norfolk Line vessel leaving port and a P&O ferry scurrying in from

France. Before we were safely across the inward channel two more English ferries and one Sea France vessel crossed our bows on their ways to or from the continent.

About a mile farther on we crossed the western exit from the port. This is separated from the eastern entrance by a long straight breakwater almost a mile in length. This gives the harassed skipper of a small boat a few minutes of composure before all his faculties need to bristle again like the hairs of a scalded cat. The westernmost exit is used by hovercraft and catamarans, which are noisier and faster than the conventional ferries. Those approaching the port can be heard from afar but they do not slow down until quite near the breakwater so one has to be very much on the *qui vive*. We had no difficulty spotting a Hoverspeed cat leaving port, after which we scuttled across the channel before a similar but inward-bound vessel snarled between the jetties behind us. By 1730 we were clear of the cross-channel traffic and able to head along the line of the misty white chalk cliffs towards Folkestone – five miles away in the increasing tranquillity of a calm, soothing, warm summer evening.

Folkestone harbour was completely devoid of water so I selected a spot off the entrance to the inner harbour to anchor in deep enough water to stay afloat all night. Harbours which dry out completely are best avoided when on passage for you can only get out again when the rising tide allows you to, and with the current spell of fine weather I wanted to be free to make progress as quickly as possible. When cruising purposefully one needs to be an opportunist, and I wanted to be in Portsmouth when the festivities commenced.

The early-morning shipping forecast was quite promising – winds northwest becoming variable 3–4 with moderate visibility – so the prospects of getting round Dungeness and perhaps as far as Eastbourne looked good.

Certainly when hauling up the anchor just before seven o'clock the morning was a dream, with the sun shining warmly from a clear blue sky. As we nosed our way round the curvature of the jetty out into the English Channel the sea was a misty flat calm with just a few widely scattered fishing boats examining their overnight pots. On a course slightly west of due south we reached Dungeness in a couple of hours with the seascape entirely our own. It took us about three-quarters of an hour before we were truly round the low-level headland into Rye Bay, with the lighthouse and nuclear power station fluttering mistily behind our ensign and the long shingle spit stretching bleakly away to starboard towards Rye harbour.

Two experiences of the past came to mind as I looked about me. The first was an unpleasant reminder of my second attempt, years ago, to sail to the Isle of Wight. This had culminated in the loss of my 16-foot YM Senior on the steeply shelving shingle less than a mile from the boundary fence of the power station. On that occasion I had anchored too close inshore and when the tide dropped her rudder had become unshipped and had floated away unseen. My attempt to get out of trouble using the outboard only for steerage had failed and we had finished up pinned by the wind onto the beach. There she settled on the flukes of an old anchor and was holed. After an anguished struggle to save the boat she became a constructive total loss and was written off by the insurance company. The second reminiscence was of being apprehended by a bustling patrol boat years later between the ness and the cliffs of Fairlight. On that occasion I was politely informed that I had strayed into a firing range and should change course to the southward for a mile or so, where we ought to be safe.

As I relived both occasions I determined that I would certainly not repeat the first of them. Regarding the second

I was not so sure – and I was not really too surprised when I spied a distant but rapidly approaching white bow wave foaming towards us. Sure enough it was another Range Patrol Boat with an almost identical message. I took a couple of snaps before innocently complying with the very sensible suggestion that we alter course to avoid being shot to pieces. The patrol boat kept a discreet eye on us until they were satisfied we were out of range and then they thundered off, bows lifting jauntily out of a frothy white wake.

By 1320 *Plover* was off Hastings pier and I calculated that in the last hour we had covered four and a half miles. Off Bexhill, full of the joys of spring, I enjoyed a bite of lunch. During the afternoon we managed to use the sails, even enjoying a forty-minute spell without the motor off Eastbourne. We passed Eastbourne pier at 1530 and to my surprised delight began rounding Beachy Head. In perfect conditions the beautiful 600-foot chalk cliff gleamed like a giant iceberg rising out of a sunny blue sea into an even bluer sky. At its foot stood its slim lighthouse, which was under our stern in about half an hour. Then we were bound for Newhaven along the line of the Seven Sisters.

Motoring along the chalky undulations of the shoreline was a sheer delight, and I was astonished to find that we were quite alone amongst all this grandeur and natural beauty, for there were no other boats abroad. Once clear of the headland the slight turbulence subsided and the sea resumed a flat calm. In not much more than an hour we arrived off Newhaven, a port I had not visited before. We needed to top up with fuel and I decided to do this at Newhaven rather than Brighton, whose marina I do not find especially appealing. Rather than spend the night in Newhaven marina I decided to anchor off the port entrance. By motoring in the following morning there would be a saving of harbour dues.

The only error in this plan, as it turned out, was that I could not obtain unleaded petrol in Newhaven without a very long walk – thus forcing me to go into Brighton anyway. However, with time to spare in the evening I checked the fuel tanks and the bilges, took a shaving off the portside locker lid to make it a better fit and had a close but unrewarding look at the erring Bidata.

Next morning when I tied the boat up in Newhaven I had needs other than fuel for I had now spent four nights on board since leaving home. Fresh water was one and rubbish disposal was another. In these environmentally conscious days the traditional philosophy and practice of 'bucket and chuck it' is not just a heresy but is also absolutely illegal. Even biodegradables can no longer be chucked over the side. Ports and marinas therefore now provide facilities for the disposal of various types of waste. I kept a plentiful supply of plastic bags on board, into which I tied my tins, plastic containers, bits of rope, and other items of waste, and these I consigned to the limited space below the cockpit floorboards. There they were certainly out of sight but they became less and less out of mind. As the days passed and the bags multiplied I was reminded of my favourite landfill sites and I was glad to be able to offload them into a convenient skip onshore. While in port it was also a pleasure to be able to use flush toilets and fresh water with relative abandon.

I tried to get my Bidata log and echo sounder device back in commission without success – I had discovered dubious wiring. The local boatyard was unable to help, and although I was able to get tiny crimp lugs the right size from the chandlery my attempts to use them without the proper pliers failed. I was more successful in getting the mast truly perpendicular, a couple of friendly boat owners giving me a hand to lengthen the forestay by adding a long shackle. By the time we had done this my planned time of departure had arrived and at 1300 I pulled the starting cord of the Mariner. We motored out of Newhaven onto a smooth, windless sea intending to call in at Brighton, six miles along, the coast for fuel and also for information about the Battle of Trafalgar bicentenary celebrations which had motivated the cruise. At this moment in time I knew very little detail about the programme or the berthing/mooring arrangements.

Once clear of the port I enjoyed a cockpit lunch in the heat of the day, wearing just a pair of shorts. This was dream boating and I counted myself lucky to be making such good progress, even though it was all courtesy of the outboard rather than the sails.

At Brighton marina we took on 31 litres of petrol and a four-litre container of outboard oil which, mixed in the ratio of 1 : 100, I hoped would be enough to get us back home. At Reception the helpful staff printed out several sheets of information for me about the programme and harbour arrangements for Portsmouth and the Solent.

Our diversion into Brighton cost us an hour and a quarter, and I hoped that we would still have time to work our way through the Looe Channel and round Selsey Bill before the tide turned against us. There did not seem to be much strength in the tide as we steered 255 degrees with no wind and the sea so calm it was almost glassy. Visibility remained something of a problem but there were no other craft in my field of vision.

In finding the Looe Channel navigational problems cropped up. At 1645 the Shoreham buoy and chimney were in transit and the Navico was holding a steady course on 255 in flat calm. I calculated we were going 6 knots. At 1800 I logged that I could not agree with the GPS, which alleged that my East Borough Head waypoint was 17 nautical miles and 119 degrees away. I continued looking for the buoy in the unhelpfully hazy conditions. Instinct and the sun told me we should change course, and at 1815 we turned westward onto 270. It was calm and misty with no buoys or other craft about. The Magellan now told me we were 19.9 nautical miles and 109 degrees away from East Borough Head. The bearings I could believe but not the distances. Five minutes later a beacon appeared on the starboard bow. This was abeam ten minutes later and after another ten minutes we had a buoy to port and I was straining to confirm that the Isle of Wight was on the bow. At 1842 I logged that the island was in fact 'clear ahead' and at 1850 that we were through the Looe channel.

We continued heading westwards into the misty track of the sun, for I had decided to make Bembridge our overnight destination. I was congratulating myself on following my hunches and pondering on the mysterious readings of the GPS when at 1915 I recorded, 'Mystifying mist – IoW has gone!' And indeed it had. A fogbank had blotted out Bembridge. We plugged on into the blue-grey misty nothingness ahead with no seamarks, no shoreline and no other craft to port, starboard or astern.

I sensed that we were not moving as we had been and, with the sun angling towards an invisible horizon, decided on a change of plan. Instead of aiming for Bembridge, which I now considered beyond our reach, we changed course so as to bring up somewhere along the western shore of Selsey Bill, probably near Bracklesham. There we would be able to anchor for the night before going into Chichester Harbour next morning. This took longer than I expected, well over half an hour, during which time visibility to port was very poor indeed while to starboard there was relative clarity. Later than expected, we closed the shore and began nosing around looking for a suitable spot to drop anchor. Once more I rued the lack of an echo sounder in working order, for we suddenly hit rocks, lots of them! Gingerly we retreated into deeper water – only to find ourselves in a veritable Sargasso Sea of dense, long trailing weed, acres of it! Again we retreated.

We felt our way tentatively along the coast until we hit bungalows and then a modern complex with a fancy roof which I guessed was probably being developed as a holiday resort including a hotel and dance hall, for loud music was travelling across the shallow water. Not wanting too loud a lullaby after a long puzzling day, I dropped the anchor over the bow half a mile or so short of the buildings. The anchor did not hold and I had to haul it up and restart the motor. When I spotted a buoy nearby I decided that that was almost certainly the best bet for the night, even though the slimy mooring did not look as though it had been used for quite a while. Anyway, thankful for the calm conditions and quite pleased that at least we were round Selsey Bill, although disappointed at not reaching the Isle of Wight, I put the kettle on, opened some tins and pulled the cork out of a bottle of wine before unrolling my sleeping bag.

I woke at 0630 sensing that all was not 100% OK. In fact we were aground on firm sand about forty yards off the low water line. I was a little concerned about the rudder blade but managed to unship it without difficulty and took the opportunity to give it a good scrub. The mist had cleared during the night and when I looked around I was not surprised to see the holiday complex where it had been last night but I was puzzled not to see the Isle of Wight on the seaward bow. Without a chart I was not much wiser – which was a shame because we were clearly not where I thought we were and I was, therefore, not feeling very wise.

I caught the general weather forecast on my wind-up Roberts radio. This predicted widespread thunderstorms with the threat of torrential downpours. Before releasing the weedy, slimy buoy which had secured us for the night I toasted some bread for breakfast, using a mini-hacksaw to slice the loaf – for one of the things I had forgotten to check aboard was a kitchen knife. I also topped up my mobile phone using my credit card.

We floated soon after 0800 and at 0920 we got under way, heading along the coast past the holiday complex. But this found us steering 240 degrees and not the 300 we would have needed had we been at or near Bracklesham. Totally mystified, a little annoyed and secretly ashamed, I began seriously to try to work out where we were and why we were where we were. I had my very small-scale chart, compass and the sun to help me. I chose to ignore the GPS, which I did not trust.

It occurred to me that if we were steering 240 with land on our starboard side then we must still be on the *east* side, not the west side, of Selsey Bill. In that case we had spent the night off or near to Bognor Regis, not Bracklesham! What must have happened was this. We must have successfully navigated the Looe Channel last night on the very last of the ebb tide. The fog bank which appeared ahead of us, blotting out the Isle of Wight, must have coincided with the change of tide, which quickly became strong enough to sweep us straight back through the aptly named Looe. Thus when we changed plans and altered course for the west coast of the Bill we were in fact steering for the eastern shoreline. This was the only explanation which seemed to me to fit the facts – improbable though it might seem.

Satisfied in my own mind, we now set off along the coast, steering 240 with a favourable tide running, I estimated, at between one and two knots. Prominent off Pagham lay a very tall metal beacon. This had no topmark so we went right up to it, hoping that it would have a name which would enable us to fix our position. It didn't. We passed it about 50 feet to port and as we drew level with it there was an almighty metallic clang and the boat stopped dead. I had been standing in the cockpit and was now pitchforked unceremoniously into the cabin where I landed as a crumpled heap. My glasses came off, my head hurt and I was conscious of blood, lots of it. Luckily I found my specs on the cabin floor and they were unbroken. I whipped up the cabin floorboards expecting the worst and was greatly relieved not to find a torrent of water gushing in, just the normal bilge. Using a handy tea towel I staunched the blood from two gashes in my forehead and took general stock of the situation. Then, satisfied that no great harm had been done to either boat or body, we were able to resume cruising, thanking our lucky stars that we had survived a head-on (no pun intended) collision with some submerged object, almost certainly concrete, at fully six miles per hour!

As we progressed along the coast my confidence as to our position became a certainty when the unmistakable outline of an RNLI launching ramp and shed appeared on a rather murky bow. This just had to be the Selsey Bill station. There were plenty of moorings in the vicinity, several of them vacant, so I decided to pick up one of them. A purple-black thunderstorm was threatening and I needed to clean up the boat and myself – and a cup of tea would not go amiss. While I was sipping reflectively in the cabin waiting for the storm to break, I wondered what it must be like to crash in a car, not at six miles per hour but at thirty or even sixty. Then, on this unhappy morn, I was astonished suddenly to see the rudder become unshipped and immediately disappear over the transom. Putting my amazement to one side for the moment, I shot into the cockpit, started the outboard with a commanding pull, dashed forward to drop the mooring buoy overboard and steer *Plover* so as to cut off the rudder, which was floating on the tide towards the piles supporting the lifeboat ramp. I managed to recapture it with inches to spare. Then, with the rudder safely back on its pintles, I forgot about my unfinished tea and headed off for the Bill. How and why the rudder became dislodged remains a mystery to me. We were afloat in deep water, the tiller was coupled up to the autopilot and the motions of the water were quite regular and not the least exceptional. I could not figure it out. But the incident taught me a lesson, and henceforth I always cleated-up the tiller with a length of shock cord when not under way.

I was surprised how quickly we reached the Bill. I was probably underestimating the strength of the rising tide, but I did appreciate that in these circumstances it ought to be safe to risk the inshore route round the sea-level headland. In fact we rounded Selsey Bill for the second time in twenty-four hours without difficulty and with considerable relief. Although we were now somewhat the worse for wear at least we had correctly worked out what had mysteriously happened the previous evening. This time everything fitted – on shore the coastguard tower on the Bill was unmistakable and the Isle of Wight, although misty, was reluctantly where it ought to be.

Now we were steering along the westernmost line of the Bill and a brisk wind and ebb tide helped us past the real and undistinguished Bracklesham Bay towards Chichester Harbour. By reference to the *CA Cruising Almanac* we avoided the sands lying off West Wittering and had a brisk tussle with a force 3 wind opposing the tide over the bar before we reached the buoys marking the channel up to Itchenor. There, with thunderstorms rumbling all around, we spotted the visitors' pontoon just before the heavens opened.

I called first of all at the local boatyard, hoping to get the autopilot repaired, but they had Friday-afternoonitis and were unable to promise help before Monday. However, the young lady in the Harbour Office was most helpful and she arranged for one of the Harbourmaster's patrolmen to come aboard the boat to see what could be done. Sure enough, such a one duly arrived within fifteen minutes. Cheerfully he re-crimped the loose wires and the echo sounder duly woke up. I was delighted, doubly so when any form of payment was refused – it was, I was assured, 'all part of the service'.

A heavy thunderstorm dominated the next forty minutes or so, after which I moved the boat upstream to a visitors' pontoon, noting the vigour of the ebb which I estimated at 2½–3 knots. That evening I dined early – I had, after all, missed lunch. I also dined well – chicken curry and spaghetti bolognaise made more palatable by a glass of red wine and followed by swiss roll, blackcurrant jam and tinned custard. Before turning in, I wrote up the log and did a bit of homework on Chichester Harbour and the bicentenary celebrations.

After a quiet night with no cramp I got a first-aider from a neighbouring motor cruiser to have a look at my swollen thumb. This was troubling me more than my other collision injuries. My forehead was beginning to heal and the whiplash was getting better by the hour but the thumb remained a truly 'sore thumb'. I was advised to bathe it as often as practicable in a strong solution of biological washing powder or liquid as hot as bearable 'as a guard against infection'. Fortunately I did have a squeezy container of biological liquid under the sink and I began the treatment forthwith, though I suspected correctly that the treatment might be worse than the disease.

At the harbourmaster's jetty I paid my dues, used the ablutions and acquired more useful information. Then we motored off for breakfast. I was disappointed that the echo sounder had died another death and after an unsuccessful attempt at anchoring I picked up a mooring not far from the Fairway buoy. There, while the kettle came to a boil, I put the mini-hacksaw to work again.

On a mild but grey morning we motored gently up to Bosham, which looked worthy of exploration. However we were politely refused permission to tie up at Bosham Quay, where berths were obviously very limited and some sort of visiting flotilla was expected. We therefore headed back towards Itchenor against the last of the flood, using the genoa to neutralise the tide. By the time we reached Chaldock, where the tide turned favourable, the broad expanse of water was alive with weekend sailors, many racing in dense fleets like flocks of geese, while hundreds of other nondescript boats were sailing for non-competitive pleasure.

Among the most popular classes were 'X' designs, Wayfarers, 420s and 470s. The Olympic classes demonstrated some fascinating sailing, leading to the capsizing of three boats. Enjoying the ideal sailing conditions in this understandably popular mecca of racing and cruising men, we crossed the harbour over to the Camber buoy, from which we turned northwards up the Thorney channel towards Emsworth. Off Mill Rythe, after two hours under sail, I furled the jib and started the motor.

Soon we were approaching Emsworth, and as it was still only mid afternoon I was reluctant to moor up. After a hurried glance at the chart in the CA *Almanac* I thought it would be a good idea to circumnavigate Hayling Island if we could get round its northern end before it dried out. This we did manage to do, and I began looking for an anchorage or mooring among the craft off Northney (Langstone). One thing puzzled me deeply – this was the busy road bridge which appeared to completely obstruct the channel and also to make the circumnavigation of Hayling Island by any boat with a mast quite impossible. I looked again at the chart but could see no bridge. I looked back the way we had come and again at the chart and still remained puzzled. Mystified, we sidled up to a couple preparing to leave their moored yacht in an inflatable. They confirmed there was no way under or past the bridge and no way of getting into Langstone Harbour except from seaward. Furthermore if I did not want to get neaped I had better scuttle back to Northney without delay.

Still unable to make sense of all this, I nevertheless took their advice and took a short cut back past Northney marina. Beyond the marina at Sweare Deep were maybe a score of deep-water moorings, all of them occupied by yachts much bigger than *Plover*. I found one which was free and put the kettle on. Before it had time to boil, however, I was hailed by the crew of a Westerly politely claiming the mooring but helpfully pointing out another vacant mooring quite near.

Over my hot sweet tea I made a determined attempt to understand my position. In the cockpit while under way I had repeatedly examined the chart without locating any bridge but I just could not believe that the Cruising Association would publish inaccurate information. I retraced my course and of course discovered that the chart was right and I was not. The bridge was there right enough and I had missed it, I believe, because it crossed the sandy colour of a drying channel and not the blue of deep water. I had made the mistake of overlooking the fact that drying channels have a habit of filling with water and becoming navigable. Silly, when you think about it. Furthermore if I had paid closer attention to the scale of the chartlet I would have realised that we were not as far round Hayling Island as I had thought we were.

On Sunday 26 June, the seventh day of the trip, we first of all motored up to Emsworth, where we tied up at the visitors' pontoon, well short of the town and marina. There we had to wait for the tide to seep into the drying harbour. When I was on the point of impatiently casting off, one of the Harbourmaster's RIBs arrived towing a casualty. To my surprise it was my good electronic Samaritan from Itchenor. He enquired about the Bidata, and when I told him it was still caput he had a quick look and agreed that ingress of water had probably sealed its fate for good.

At Emsworth we grounded some fifty yards short of the public landing stage and had to wait for the best part of an hour for sufficient water before we could get ashore. During that time I picked the brains of a local fisherman, who was reluctant to believe that we were less than a week out of Ipswich in a boat which he obviously considered too small, unseaworthy and dubiously manned. Emsworth proved to be a convenient and compact shopping centre and I bought eight litres of petrol and a general-purpose kitchen knife which was going to save me a fortune in hacksaw blades and breadcrumbs. I also bought a gas lighter for the cooker, various provisions, mostly in tins, and some batteries for the camera. It would have been nice to spend more time in Emsworth but we had really come in here for business reasons and I was anxious to complete this first leg of the trip by reaching Portsmouth.

I hurried back to *Plover*, where the harbour had now come to life with the inflow of water. People, fishermen, holidaymakers and boats were everywhere. My plan was to make haste downriver to the Chichester bar and then take advantage of the ebb tide to Portsmouth, where I anticipated we might have problems finding a mooring although to my great surprise, and untypically, we had arrived a day or two early! We made good speed to the harbour entrance, helped by a kindly NNE breeze which nicely filled the genoa. Over the bar we joined a crowd of craft all leaving the channels, creeks and marinas of the harbour in the warm sunshine. Most of them seemed to be heading for the Isle of Wight, but we took a westerly course past Langstone harbour.

3

Trafalgar bicentennial celebrations

As we approached Portsmouth my pulse quickened when I felt certain that there really was an aircraft carrier looming mistily on the horizon off the Isle of Wight. Then there was another, and as we approached the Solent I was thrilled to see long lines of anchored warships and tall ships becoming nearer and clearer. The sea was a bit lumpy but I steered over toward the island in order to take photographs. I got some good shots of a huge Russian three-master before being warned by a security patrol that we were approaching a prohibited area – I had read that there was a 400-metre exclusion zone round all the anchored vessels. I now had to make a decision – either go to the Isle of Wight and anchor there for the duration of the festivities, probably off Ryde, or go into Portsmouth. I chose the latter, where we would certainly have more protection in the event of bad weather and where there ought to be a better chance and choice of moorings. Portsmouth, Southsea and Gosport would also be the focal points of activity.

I was glad that we did, for as we made for the harbour entrance we found ourselves in a wild melee of craft similarly confined like ourselves to the official navigational channels, some heading inshore, others outward bound, some sailing, others under power. There were tall ships, warships, Isle of Wight ferries and cross-channel ferries, fishing boats, hovercraft, motor cruisers, day boats, yachts and sailing boats of infinite variety, together with a prominent sprinkling of protective patrol boats. It was all very colourful and hugely exciting – rather like being in a dinghy race. It was necessary to maintain a constant, all-round watch and exercise continuous judgement as to the probable movements of other craft, both adjacent and distant. The closing speed of some of the larger craft under full power took some getting used to and at one point *Plover* found herself on a collision course with the TS *Royalist*, which was bearing down upon us uncompromisingly at a disturbing rate of knots. Needless to say it was *Plover* which had to take hasty evasive action, accompanied by an orgasmic surge of adrenalin. We sheered off to port to avoid crossing in front of the big sailing ship and possibly getting run down. You can imagine my amazement, therefore, when a hovercraft roared out of nowhere, sending us rocking as she passed close under our stern and cheekily whizzed straight across the bows of the training ship we had just given way to.

Off Southsea I picked up repeated shoutings from our starboard quarter. They were coming from a Pandora sailing boat, a crew member of which was energetically waving aloft a plastic five-litre fuel can. Guessing what the problem was, we closed alongside. The skipper asked if we had some unleaded petrol to spare as he didn't think he had enough on board to get back to base. I rummaged into the cockpit locker and happily passed over one of my containers and then resumed focusing on the gap between Gosport and Portsmouth.

It was many years since I had sailed into Portsmouth, and the 170-metre Millennium Tower did not then exist. I must say that I think it is a most attractive enhancement of the waterfront. I waited until there were a few feet of clear water ahead of us and then pointed the digital camera in its direction. As we sailed into Portsmouth I was on a real 'high', for there was so much to see. In addition to the new tower, which dominated the waterfront like a huge spinnaker, and the general bustle on the water there was HMS *Warrior*, the first steam-driven ironclad warship, in her dry dock, a glimpse of the masts of HMS *Victory* and the much-filmed *Grand Turk*, and a score of tall ships already berthed two and three deep.

As the inner harbour broadened out and mothballed warships multiplied I was again hailed by the Pandora, which had come up astern of us. They handed me back my plastic container, by no means empty, together with a couple of pounds and their thanks. When I enquired about possible moorings they suggested we follow them to their sailing club where there were certainly moorings available. We tucked in behind them and duly arrived at Hardway Sailing Club on the Gosport side. Here there were small-craft moorings marked on the chart, and this was where we had been hopefully heading for anyway! I declined space on the pontoon in favour of a swinging mooring but had to move when a friendly South African came over to tell me I had picked up a marker buoy. After a cup of coffee together I took the boat off to find another mooring, during which operation I unfortunately saw the boathook go over the side and descend like a metal harpoon towards the bottom. Worse was to come. While dithering whether to go onto the pontoon or find another buoy, we touched bottom on the falling tide and were unable to get off. We dried out completely, not refloating until after dark. One good thing – I noticed that the Bidata seemed to be working again, though how well remained to be seen. Finally I got up twice during the night to try to locate the cause of a strong smell of petrol, particularly when lying down.

In the morning we motored over to the sailing club pontoon, where I made it my first job to tackle the petrol problem – a faulty jubilee clip. I then emptied all our spare fuel containers into the main tanks – eleven litres into the port tank and ten into starboard. I learned that the security gate at the end of the pontoon would not be unlocked until 10 a.m. so I had breakfast. In the clubhouse I found no officials but a few helpful and curious members and with their cooperation I was able to enjoy a shower and wash my dirty clothes. Right next to the club there was a chandlery where I was able to buy a replacement boathook, an extensible one, and also swap Camping Gaz cylinders, removing from my mind the worry of running out. But I had no luck with the erring Bidata.

After lunch we motored gently down to Haslar Creek, the original one where the naval hospital still exists to which sailors were traditionally sent, knowing that they would not be needing a paddle any more. It was my hope to find a visitors' berth there for an hour or so while I paid a quick visit to the accident and emergency department of the famous hospital about my thumb, which was not mending as it should. The plan misfired when the marina mooring master insisted that I would have to pay a minimum of £6.

Unpleased, we motored out of the busy harbour and joined the fleet of assorted pleasure craft scurrying along the coast to and beyond Gilkicker Point. It was dress-rehearsal day for the Royal Review of the Fleet commemorating the bicentenary of the Battle of Trafalgar and the whole of the Solent was dominated by three endless lines of warships with a few tall ships and an Isle of Wight ferryboat incongruously anchored conspicuously in the middle of them. At Spithead there were a couple of aircraft carriers, one of them the massive nuclear-powered *Charles de Gaulle*, but most of the rest that I saw were fleet auxiliaries of one sort or another with a few frigates scattered amongst them.

The days of battleships, cruisers and destroyers were clearly over. Over eighty countries had sent representative vessels. Helicopters clattered about overhead and down below scores of patrolling rigid inflatables, wearing the insignia of the harbourmaster, the police, the coastguard, the Boat Squadron or RYA, ensured that no unauthorised craft strayed nearer than 400 metres to the men-of-war. Conspicuous orange buoys marked out the exclusion zones while in the designated small-craft anchorage areas early birds had already selected vantage points for the events of the morrow. In *Plover* we conducted our own modest review of the fleet, motoring towards Southampton Water in the warm sunshine.

On our return passage five frigates steamed past in line-ahead formation between the anchored naval craft, followed by modest fly-pasts of aircraft at high level and helicopters, more impressively, at low level. Our preview of the real thing was completed when the Antarctic Survey Ship HMS *Endurance* overtook us as we passed the Millennium Tower. This was the ship from whose bridge the Queen and Prince Philip were due to review the fleet next day. She looked colourfully spic and span after a refit.

Instead of going back to Hardway we explored the dockyard, where a huge Russian three-master and the *Grand Turk* were lying. Then we crossed the harbour over to the Portchester channel to find a mooring for the night – in a creek opposite Portchester castle with the approval of the local mooring master. The evening was blazing hot and after stringing my laundry along the boom I could not resist the opportunity for a nap. Then before cooking my evening meal I had another look at two continuing irritations.

There were still occasional whiffs of petrol, so I cut a longer piece of plastic pipe to replace a weepy length and I discovered that one of the Bidata crimps was not pushed properly home. Both jobs seemed as though they might be successful: the smell disappeared and the echo sounder gave a credible readout.

As the warm daylight faded from a sky full of rich autumn colours the skipper of a neighbouring yacht rowed over socially. He said that he would be early away in the morning for his boat was one of the three hundred or so private pleasure craft selected to take part in the royal sail-past. He had won the honour in a competition!

On the morning of the royal review the early-morning forecast was very disappointing – winds E or ENE 5–6 decreasing 4–5 – and the general forecast for Portsmouth was for heavy thundery showers towards evening. I decided this was a good day to be a landlubber. But from our present position opposite Portchester we were going to be right out of the action. Accordingly we quickly scuttled across the breadth of the harbour, back to Hardway, where we picked up a mooring in the lee of a couple of mothballed frigates.

After mooring up I then appreciated the difficulties I was going to face using the Avon Redstart, especially if returning late at night. Accordingly I moved the boat to the sailing club pontoon where, surprisingly, there was space. Now I was able to use the clubhouse again with its showers and other facilities. On the pontoon I assembled the folding bicycle and gave it a test run on the road. Then I packed a rucksack and pedalled off to Gosport and Gilkicker Point to see the fun.

The waterfront at Gosport was thick with people – it was a choice location from which to see the royal party's arrival. Unfortunately they had already left by the time I got there so after a few minutes I cycled off in the direction of Gilkicker Point. There I joined crowds of people picnicking among the sand dunes which overlooked one of the designated anchorage areas. This was chock-a-block with small craft, many of which had been there all night. I had

▲ 'Has been'?

◀ Leaving the
Orwell

▶
Rounding the
North Foreland

▲ Bosham

◀ Approaching Portsmouth and the Trafalgar bicentennial celebrations

▶ Sea Cadets beating retreat past HMS *Victory*

◄ Departing
Cowes

► St Michael's
Mount

◄ The Longships
lighthouse,
off Land's End

► Trevose Head

▶ Lifeboatman
James comes
aboard off
Boscastle
(*photo:
Mike England*)

Oh happy day!
(*photo:
Mike England*)
▼

▲
Under tow

◀
Returning
to the boat
at Barry

been tempted to join them but had decided I would see more as a landlubber. While waiting for things to happen I chatted to a local resident, who was very well informed.

The review of the assembled fleet was, from the Gilkicker point of view, definitely not spectator sport at its best. In fact it was a damp squib. The *Endurance* led a procession of eight assorted craft up one side of the Solent and back down the other in between the lines of warships. The nearest of these must have been at least a kilometre offshore, beyond the masts of the anchored pleasure craft. Without binoculars no hint of human activity could be detected either on the royal craft or on the respectful naval vessels – no waving could be seen, no doffing of caps, no manning of the yards, no cheers could be heard, no pipes called. The eight unpretentious ships, including the *Grand Turk*, passed quietly by and into the misty distance where storm clouds were gathering ominously.

When the reviewing flotilla passed by on its return towards Portsmouth on the Isle of Wight side of the Solent it was even farther away and I decided to head back myself. As nothing in particular was now going on I took the opportunity to have a look at the High Street in Gosport. Surprisingly I found a cycle shop so I bought the items needed to make my old Bickerton fully serviceable – a pump, a bell and a lighting set. Almost next door happened to be a Help the Aged charity shop. A firm believer that charity begins at home, I managed to help the aged person I know best to a smart pair of shell trousers and a pair of training type shoes. These I hoped would serve as deck shoes to replace the ones I had been wearing for more than a year, the soles of which I no longer really trusted.

Thunderstorms looked imminent and it occurred to me that with a break in the official programme this might be a very good time to pay the nearby Haslar Naval Hospital a visit to see what they thought of my thumb. Unfortunately

I was misdirected repeatedly on my way there and a journey which should have been less than a mile became at least ten. To make matters worse as I pedalled round in a huge circle, often in dense traffic, three miles of heavy rain began to fall.

After dropping in at the hospital reception desk it was clear that my plan was going to work. There was only one other outpatient there and I scarcely had time to go to the toilet before I was examined by a nurse. She suspected a fracture and sent me to X-ray, where her suspicions were confirmed. The end segment of the right thumb was dramatically displaced. The nurse gave me a local anaesthetic and pressed the 'undo' button before sending me back to radiography. A second celluloid showed all segments of the digit neatly back in good naval line-ahead formation, and after a cup of tea I was joyfully dismissed. It had all taken less than an hour. I jumped on the bicycle full of the joys of spring – my plan had worked and my thumb was repaired. But spring rapidly turned to autumn. I had covered only about a half-mile when one of the bicycle pedals became unscrewed and clattered into the gutter, which was now swilling with water as another thundershower broke. Furious as I was, I had to admit I was not all that surprised. I had had this trouble several times in the past, most recently on my trip to Norwich a couple of years ago. Unable to rethread the pedal I half walked, half scooted into Gosport, where I left the machine in the alley leading to the High Street cycle shop where I had bought the pump and lighting set.

I now checked how and when I could get a bus back to Hardway. Then I went to the Castle Inn to reflect on the events of the day and to buy myself a lager and a meal. As dusk descended I joined the crowds on the waterfront opposite the Millennium Tower, managing to find a ringside perch on the harbour wall. A simulated battle accompanied by *son et lumière* was scheduled to take place at nightfall. I'm sure that it did take place but unfortunately for those hundreds of us expectantly gathered at Gosport the simulation and subsequent firework display might as well have been at Cape Trafalgar itself for all the action that we saw. In the very far distance we did hear periodic and fairly frequent explosions, and there were two faint pools of misty light, one red and one blue, out at sea. Then after a very long time the fireworks began. They went on for a very long time and must have been quite exceptional and really spectacular for those near enough to enjoy them. But for those of us at Gosport the squib was truly damp for we were disappointingly miles away. The massive chrysanthemum bursts which repeatedly opened up off Southsea were merely for us the size of five-penny pieces in the night sky. We had obviously picked a very poor vantage point for this climax of the celebrations. And very fine they apparently were, for the newspapers next morning carried superb colour photographs of a quite breathtaking event.

There was one major consolation for those of us wrong-footed at Gosport, however. We escaped the mammoth traffic jams and chaos on the other side of the water when the show was all over. Apparently vast numbers suffered well into the small hours, in cars and coaches, at rail stations and on ferries. For my part I made sure that I was waiting at the nearby bus terminus when the last bus pulled in.

The Fleet Review and Trafalgar commemoration was now over, but in two days' time an International Festival of the Sea was due to start, featuring of course the tall ships now here in force. I decided to stay on. Before taking the bus into Gosport I spent next morning doing some leisurely carpentry. I was able to make a table extension, which made my meal times much more relaxing and pleasant, and also made writing up the log less of a tedious effort. I also had another look at the echo sounder, which puzzled me by only displaying the top half of the digits. I found that by applying pressure to the VDU I was able to bring up a complete readout. I tightened up the casing.

After lunch I took the bus into Gosport and went straight to the cycle shop, which I hoped would have repaired my pedal. To my chagrin I found the shop closed, together with many others – it was early-closing day! Annoyed and disappointed at not having two wheels at my disposal, I took the ferry over to Portsmouth and used my two legs to explore the waterfront from Southsea to the dockyard, dodging the occasional heavy showers. After a jacket potato in the historic Still & Western pub I returned by ferry and bus to the boat at Hardway. This had been a rather flat but exhausting day.

I succeeded in recovering the folding cycle on the morning of the first day of the International Festival of the Sea. To solve my longstanding problem with the right-hand pedal I had a new crankshaft fitted for £15. Then I took the bike with me on the ferry over to Portsmouth in company with the hundreds of others who were all heading for the IFOS in the dockyard.

As a senior citizen my ticket for the first day of the IFOS cost me just £10. For this nominal sum I was able to go aboard HMS *Warrior* and HMS *Victory* and see the ill-fated *Mary Rose* undergoing the last years of her water-based preservation treatment. Glass-encased, her remains are being continually sprayed with a waxy solution to impregnate her timbers. Nearby was the separate museum where many salvaged relics were on display, and the absorbing question as to the real cause of the coming to grief of the Tudor warship was intriguingly posed but not answered. Had there been time I could also have looked over goodness knows how many tall ships plus the little *Pickle*, which had brought the good news of triumph and the bad news of death home from Spain two hundred years ago. I did spend time, however, listening to some lively sea shanties, and elsewhere to the music and antics of a superb band, the Jive Aces. At one of the quayside market stalls I bought some very useful and very cheap tools for the boat and the galley. Then at the end of the day, after a bargain day out, I caught a ferry back to Gosport and cycled back to the boat well satisfied.

4

The Isle of Wight

It was time to move on, so on the morning of 1 July, day twelve of this adventure, I dismantled the Bickerton and prepared *Plover* for the sea. Before leaving the harbour we called at Camper & Nicholson's marina for fuel but when I saw that they were charging £1.00 a litre for unleaded petrol when the filling station price was 88p I refused to pay and we motored away, bound for Cowes.

The morning forecast had predicted southwesterly winds force 4–5 with drizzle and possible fog patches. To start with we had the last of the ebb tide with us and we made good progress under power. Approaching Stokes Bay we lost the tide and I unfurled the jib. After some thought I decided to haul up the mainsail as well. I knew that I would have to be quick, for sea room was limited. It was a bad decision. With an unreliable Tillerpilot I had the greatest difficulty in getting the boat to stay head to wind while we were being set onshore by a forceful current. In the end, with an unfriendly shore uncomfortably close, I had to sail offshore with the mainsail only halfway up the mast. A quite vicious tide was now running, and by the time I had the mainsail properly set *Plover* had been swept a couple of miles back to Gilkicker Point.

We spent the next one and a half, maybe two hours,

close-hauled and stemming the tide. *Plover* was not very happy in these conditions and headway over the ground was painfully slow. Time was not a problem but in the end I acknowledged that we had spent long enough on this particular point of the learning curve and I started the motor and furled both sails. In murky rain and drizzle we slowly crossed the Solent over to the island with friendly nods in the directions of Osborne House and the old castle at East Cowes. There were no particularly interesting craft lying off Cowes and, finding the buoyed channel without difficulty, we motored up the Medina River between the boatyards, marinas, and various marine enterprises until we reached the Folly Inn. This has been made popular by a chain of visitors' pontoons which have been moored in the middle of the river. Here the surroundings are pleasantly rural and the pub helps to make this an attractive port of call for visiting yachtsmen. We tied up there for an hour or so and then, after picking the brains of local sailors, decided to continue on up to Newport, where we would be able to moor up for the night and obtain the petrol we needed from a convenient filling station.

At Newport we tied up at the town quay as rain poured down. As quickly as I could I rigged the boom cover, for this just about doubles the dry habitable space on board. My first priority now was fuel and I was lucky to find a filling station about a quarter of a mile away. I strapped three five-litre containers onto my collapsible trolley and made two trips to the garage, adding over 30 litres to the tanks. Unfortunately, although I had dipped the tanks, I overfilled the second tank and about half a litre of petrol ended up in the bilges. With the cockpit floorboards up and all lockers open I sponged this up immediately and then did so again with detergent. But the smell of petrol remained and it was obvious that I would not be able to do any cooking that night.

This was one of the low points of the trip. It was dark, it was raining, the boom tent although protective was also claustrophobic, the boat was a mess from end to end, and the smell of petrol was overpowering. I was tired and I was hungry. I was still affected by whiplash from the collision and my bandaged thumb was still troublesome. Most of all I was annoyed for bringing most of this misery upon myself. To add insult to injury my friend Rudi had told me over the phone earlier in the evening that he was thinking of selling his much-admired 21-foot sailing boat and I had immediately responded by asking for first refusal. From my present miserable perspective, at this particular juncture, the attractions his boat offered seemed irresistible – more space, more headroom, a proper galley and toilet and an inboard diesel engine using cheap, tax-free, universally obtainable, less flammable fuel as opposed to an awkwardly situated outboard motor thirstily golloping down unleaded petrol at inflated prices. Likewise the advantages of a glass-fibre construction rather than ageing marine ply were painfully obvious – bone-dry bilges, no leaks through the cabin roof, the annual refit with a damp rag in place of countless hours of carpentry, filling, priming, undercoating, gloss-finishing and varnishing, all separated by reels of masking tape. Yes, I am afraid I have to admit that late on a rainy, smelly, disorganised and cramped evening I would have swapped *Plover* with little hesitation.

Brooding on the limitations and inadequacies of *Plover* was solving nothing, however. Unable to cook on board because of the reek of petrol, I hurried into the nearby town centre a few minutes before ten o'clock hoping to find a fish and chip shop open. I was lucky to find a takeaway still serving and I ordered chicken and chips. Possibly because the shop was on the point of closing, the portions I was served were enormous, much more than I could eat even when washed down with a glass of wine. I thoughtfully saved half of the chicken for the following day. Now I was ready for bed but when I zipped up my sleeping bag I found that, with my head just above bilge level, the reek of petrol was still overpoweringly strong – an appropriate ending, I suppose, for a stinking day! It was a wonder that my inflammatory thoughts did not detonate an explosion.

Of course I had a spell of cramp in both legs during the night but by morning the smell of petrol was much diminished and I felt it safe to brew a cup of tea – though my new gas lighter wouldn't work at first. The 0530 forecast did not cheer me up – winds southwesterly 4–5, visibility moderate with fog patches. The filling station opened early and I made one more trip there with my five-litre containers to top up, in fact to nearly overfill, the starboard tank. I now had more than 65 litres on board. In checking the fuel system I found I was able to tighten up a couple of jubilee clips.

We motored away from Newport at 1100, having spent the morning getting the boat back to rights and paying a £3.50 'short stay' mooring fee. We sailed back downriver using the jib as far as the Folly Inn, where we found space on one of the pontoons. Here we would not be trapped by the tide; at Newport we were restricted to maybe five hours around high water when it was possible to get away. Initially I paid £3 here for a short stay, which enabled me to have lunch with a lager – followed, therefore, by forty winks. Then I got busy on the boat, completing its restoration from the night before and then seizing the four shrouds with the new pliers I had bought at the Portsmouth IFOS. I also went round the boat sealing leaks in the cabin roof and elsewhere.

My short stay soon expired and I had to make a decision. Even here in protected waters it was blowing quite hard and also raining from time to time so when the mooring master's jolly boat came round again I cheerfully paid an additional £2 for the night. Next I got busy writing up the log of the past three days but shortly a friendly and inquisitive skipper hailed me from the pontoon. He was a retired Lieutenant Commander RN, talkative and widely experienced. He was very interested in *Plover*, which did tend to stand out, rather like my sore thumb, among the big, gleaming white, glass-fibre cruisers. On hearing of my troubles with my equipment he volunteered eagerly to have a look at the Bidata, which, after a while, he pronounced OK except for the paddle wheel. I was grateful but only cautiously optimistic. I happened to see the friendly commander again briefly in Yarmouth a few days later and he enquired about the echo sounder. I took the opportunity to tell him that I now knew why he was retired from the navy because the echo sounder was still not working! I assumed, tongue-in-cheek, that he had jumped before he was pushed.

My little boat was, naturally I suppose, attracting attention simply because it was different – it was a sailing boat, it was small, it was painted green, the Orwell Yacht Club ID on her transom indicated she was from 'foreign parts', and she did not seem to have much of a crew. When I went over to the Folly Inn after frying up some more of last night's takeaway, I was sitting quietly enjoying a lager with lime when a skipper and his family introduced themselves saying, 'Hello, we saw you at Itchenor' – thus initiating a pleasant chat during which they quizzed me about my trip while I tapped into their local knowledge.

The inland waters forecast next morning wasn't much of an improvement – winds were to be west or southwest force 4, occasionally 5 later. Nevertheless I made preparations to move on, and at 0830 we cast off in calm conditions. It took us an hour to sail under the jib to and through Cowes and into the Solent.

We soon became exposed to a vigorous blow and a lumpy sea. With only the genoa set it was impossible to point westwards towards the narrows and Hurst Castle so I furled the jib and started the motor. From the middle of the Solent we headed obliquely back towards the island. Once close enough to find a lee we made good progress, helped by a fair tide. I was now resolved to target Yarmouth, hoping that we would not there be welcomed by one of their 'Harbour Full' signs.

I was relieved that there was space for us inside the harbour, though it was pretty crowded. We arrived just after noon and were allocated a berth at the western end of the harbour. From there it was possible to jump ashore and then walk into town in about fifteen minutes. As I had some serious shopping to do I decided to pump up the dinghy and row over to the harbour facilities. These are excellent, with clinically clean toilets and showers and laundry machines. While these latter spun and tumbled my plentiful dirty clothing I stocked up with provisions even though a Lloyds TSB cash dispenser gobbled up one of my credit cards.

I returned to the boat to have a nap. Refreshed, I had another go at curing an irritating fuel seepage from one of the fuel lines and then did some cosmetic undercoating around the cabin. I had now been on passage for exactly two weeks so I next spent some time getting the accounts and paperwork up to date. Then I made the last of the Newport takeaway chicken the basis of a third evening meal – this time served with marrowfat peas and mashed potatoes.

The next three days were spent weather-bound at Yarmouth. For most of that time it was blowing force 6 or more. The morning of 4 July was particularly eventful. At

1130 the sound of maroons riveted attention around the town and harbour and shortly afterwards the lifeboat left harbour and roared off towards the Needles, later to return escorting a stricken yacht. At noon Solent coastguards issued a securitay warning on channel 16 of squalls imminent in the Solent with winds of 35 knots. On channel 16 I also picked up the launches of the Lymington and Cowes lifeboats and a pan-pan dialogue with a yacht with a suspected fire on board which later turned out to be an engine overheating. Two days later the Yarmouth lifeboat was called out again.

While stuck on the Isle of Wight I did a number of repair and improvement jobs around the boat, the most important of which was to take *Plover* over to the scrubbing posts. I wanted to see what damage, if any, the boat had suffered in the collision off Pagham nearly two weeks ago and I was curious to see how effective the antifouling was. Two senior citizens on a 25-foot Westerly with whom I had become friends gave me a hand getting the boat over there at the top of the tide. While waiting for the boat to take the ground, I hailed one of the patrolling harbourmaster's launches. My freshwater tank had run out so I wondered if help could be obtained. No problem! A young New Zealander on a working holiday kindly took my flexible water carrier over to the fuel berth and returned it to me after a few minutes full of cups of tea, cooking water, washing-up water and water for personal hygiene purposes.

When *Plover* settled on her bilge keels I put on my gumboots and grovelled about inquisitively on the mud and gravel beneath her. With great relief I was unable to detect any damage due to the Pagham incident. I was horrified, however, by the number of barnacles encrusting the forward section of the hull and I scraped these off as best I could using the back of the brush I carry on board. Disturbingly I found that the paddle wheel was not only clogged with barnacles but, more importantly, had several of its small blades missing. I cleaned off the barnacles but clearly it was never going to work again. When the boat refloated I had a terrible time trying to get away from the scrubbing posts in the strong wind and flooding tide. The Avon, streamed astern, fouled one of the posts and we grounded again, lying across the wind. I tried everything to get free but in the end just had to be patient and wait for sufficient water to give us essential sea room. When we did make it back to the mooring Graham and David turned out in friendly fashion to take my lines. With more rain threatening I had to rig the boom cover again before eating and retiring.

Another useful thing I did while waiting for the weather to clear was to visit the local surgery to confirm that all was well with my thumb. This was situated in a small bungalow which was jam-packed with senior citizens, and I felt almost young and unwrinkled again when I looked around – until a young mother insisted I take her seat! A cheerful nurse had a look at my right hand and reassured me that there was nothing to worry about. The fact that it was still swollen and that I could not bend the end segment was simply nature improvising its own splint. In this way the healing process could continue, but this could take six weeks or more.

I spent the final afternoon of my stay on the island cycling to Alum Bay on the other side of the island. I managed to assemble the Bickerton in record time and, for once, had no problems with it. The round trip was a good ten hilly miles. Back on the boat I was invited aboard *Sumara* for a final cup of tea and chat with Graham and David. The winds were easing down and we all expected to get away in the morning.

High water on Friday 8 July was at 1232, after which our westward course would be helped by an ebb tide. The day started beautifully with a crystal-clear blue sky and rapidly became pleasantly warm without a breath of wind. The forecast, however, was for northwesterlies force 4–5. During the morning, while waiting for the tide, I was feverishly busy. The rains of recent days had shown that the lightweight boom cover would be a better fit if it had more eyelets so I hammered in some extras. That done, it seemed sensible to check the heavyweight cover, a rather unmanageable affair, in case we had any more protracted bad weather. At last, with the bicycle folded and stowed, we were ready to cast off and motor over to the harbour office to pay our dues, fill up with water and dispose of the last of our rubbish.

At 1240 we left the harbour and headed westwards to exit the Solent. By now it was cloudy and I soon slipped a pair of trousers over my shorts. In thirty minutes we were through the narrows off Hurst Castle with a choice of a direct course through the Needles channel towards Weymouth or the longer, safer option clinging loosely to the coastline of Christchurch Bay. Bearing in mind the forecast I erred on the side of discretion rather than valour. It was disappointing that this meant that we would not see the stacks of the Needles close up. I would love to have got a more recent shot of the lighthouse, even though the addition of a helicopter landing platform has disfigured it. As we turned away from the broken chalks of the promontory they gradually shrank in size on the horizon from distant to virtually invisible. More to the point was the fact that our course, curving round Christchurch Bay, allowed us to get some help from the wind, and for three hours we motor-sailed pleasantly offshore with the genoa unfurled. It was great to be out of harbour and sailing again.

Rather than take shelter in yet another harbour, Poole, we made for Handfast Point and Studland Bay, where I hoped we could lie at anchor overnight reasonably quietly. This would save us an hour's steaming this evening and another hour tomorrow morning. As we approached the Old Harry rocks we got drawn into a vicious race which obliged us to fight our way round the headland and into the chalky, picturesque tranquillity of this Dorset anchorage.

We finished sailing for the day unusually early but I was well pleased that we were on the move again and poised to cover more mileage tomorrow. We shared the bay with perhaps a score of other craft, which number gradually reduced as day sailors presumably weighed anchor to return to Poole. I found plenty to do pottering around the boat and gave myself a refresher course on the GPS.

5

Westward Ho!

After a quiet night, the alarm setting on my mobile phone made sure that I did not miss the 0535 shipping forecast, which was quite a good one – inland waters should enjoy northerly winds force 3 or 4 becoming variable 3 or less. If this actually happened, with any luck we should be able to reach Weymouth today with perhaps a lunch break in Lulworth Cove. That would be fantastic, and would fulfil one of my longstanding ambitions to anchor in the classic little cove.

With the predicted winds it ought to have been possible to sail out of Studland Bay, southwards to Peveril Point and then along the coast to Weymouth. In practice when I decked the anchor there was scarcely any wind but I kept the motor quiet in the expectation that the brisk northerlies which were forecast would at least start stirring. They didn't, and after an hour of pleasantly disappointing ghosting I turned to the Mariner outboard to get us out of Studland Bay, round Old Harry and his equally chalky Wife, and then southward for Swanage Bay and Peveril Point.

The winds remained on the light side throughout the very pleasant day during which we motor-sailed along the cliffs, the rolling downs and the headlands of Dorset. We passed Swanage and then edged round the headlands of Peveril Point and St Albans Head with unspiteful equanimity. Off Worbarrow a light breeze sprang up so I stopped the motor and tried to sail, hoping to nip into Lulworth. The breeze quickly died, however, and I reached for the starting cord. But the motor refused to start. There had been no hint of any trouble up to that time and we had plenty of fuel. I did nothing, and we drifted gently for about half an hour, after which I had another pull on the outboard. This time it started, though a little reluctantly, so I thought it wise to keep it going and make sure we got to Weymouth. If there were more trouble there would be little chance of any help in Lulworth Cove, which was not likely to be exactly bristling with boatyards and marinas.

We now steered due west for Weymouth with thunderstorms menacing. The engine behaved itself, though keeping me on tenterhooks, and got us to Weymouth by early evening. I got the mainsail down while we still had sea room, which was just as well for the harbour itself was unbelievably crowded and the farther one penetrated the more the boats were rafted up – four, five and even six deep.

I made to raft up on the starboard side, and as we glided in the engine failed and would not restart so that I had to shout for a fend off. A harbourmaster's launch soon attended us with the offer of a berth on the opposite side of the harbour. The young skipper was very obliging, even whipping out the spark plug before moving us across the harbour, where we rafted up outside only two other craft. That done we relaxed contentedly in the warm sunshine before having an early evening meal – we had missed lunch due to the engine failure off Worbarrow.

Saturday evening proved to be pretty lively in Weymouth. The congestion of boats on the water was incredible. Two imitation tall ships catering for day trippers were conspicuous amongst the rafted yachts and motor cruisers, the fishing trawlers, the many diving boats and the swarms of small open day boats. Along both banks of the harbour hundreds of boating types and holidaymakers jostled in, out of and between the many bars, pubs and restaurants. In the main street I was surprised to find a supermarket open so when I returned to the boat I was laden down with heavy plastic bags in both hands containing mostly tins and drinks containers. As a mellow dusk faded into semi-darkness a firework display commenced across the water. I quite liked Weymouth.

It was now nearly three weeks since we had left Ipswich, and despite the unforeseen time lost on the Isle of Wight we were now doing fairly well. The next headland to round was Portland Bill, which would let us into Lyme Bay. But in order to achieve this I first needed to get the outboard motor back into reliable commission. Happily the help I needed was only a hundred yards away. At Bussell's chandlery the owner was confident that our trouble was in the carburettor and he readily came aboard to prove his point – finding water in the fuel and some grot in the carb itself. I was delighted to have had the problem dealt with so promptly and so quickly, for we were now able to continue. Although I still had 50 litres of fuel in the tanks I felt it wise to fill up where I conveniently could, and at roadside not marina prices. In Weymouth this meant that I had to walk a generous mile to the nearest garage.

It was 1220 when we slipped our lines and motored out into the warm sunny bay, where the winds remained light. Our passage up the coast past the vast, empty and uninviting Portland Harbour, home to HM's only floating prison and destined to be one of the venues for the Olympic sailing events in 2012, was uneventful and almost without the company of any other craft. We arrived a little nervously at 1400, exactly right for rounding the Portland Bill and avoiding the infamous race.

Half an hour later we were well out into Lyme Bay, steering as near to 290 as the wind would allow. This course took us obliquely across the bay and kept both mainsail and jib drawing nicely for the best part of three hours until the winds fell light, and at 1720 I started the motor. Our course had taken us out of sight of land, though this would no doubt have been obvious had visibility been better. We had been sailing in a pretty relaxed way for the sheer pleasure of it and I spent a period in mid afternoon enjoying brief catnaps in the warm postprandial sunshine. Once clear of the Bill I did not see any other craft for the whole of the afternoon. I therefore had no precise idea where we were going to make landfall. Nor was I much bothered, for I figured we would find an overnight anchorage in the vicinity of either Exmouth or Torbay.

I was a bit disturbed when at 1815 the Mariner just suddenly stopped. After switching petrol tanks she started again, to my great relief. We approached the shore in poor visibility with no landmarks, no seamarks and no other craft to help us. Eventually the blur of the coast gradually became unmistakable though it was of low altitude and without distinguishing features. We continued on our way, closing the shore, and eventually spied a couple of yachts hugging the coast as they motored north. Realising that we either had to follow them or take their reciprocal course I decided to cut off the leading boat in order to get a fix. This took perhaps ten minutes or so, and when I throttled back to enquire where we were exactly, I almost wished I hadn't. 'Seaton in Devon – in the northern hemisphere!' came back a sarcastic and scathing harpoon of a reply from under a peaked cap. I writhed as my tiny residue of pride was punctured. I had never even heard of Seaton and it certainly was not marked on my small-scale chart. 'So how far is Exmouth?' I enquired almost impudently. 'About ten miles,' I learned. 'Where you come from, then?' next came a suspicious enquiry, as though I might not know the answer and, if I did, it was probably wrong. 'Weymouth, today,' I replied. The helmsman's tone changed ever so slightly, 'Oh, that's not too bad for a small boat, I suppose.' There was a pause, then, 'We're going back into Seaton but we can't get over the bar before ten o'clock – you can follow us if you like. Or you can anchor in the bay.' We did follow them, but only as far as Beer Head, where I sized up the situation and decided to do the latter.

In the bay and under the cliffs the anchor twice failed to hold in the deep, clear but dark brown water so we moved to a mooring nearby where we were advised we would be alright until the tripper boats came out in the morning.

The twenty-second day of the trip started superbly well – a clear blue windless sky with a forecast of 30 Celsius and a Devon Radio forecast of a 'dry week' ahead. Although we would not have a fair tide until mid afternoon I knew that we must get off our mooring before the working boats arrived. After consulting the tidal atlas I found that there was no real strength in the tides hereabout so we might as well make what progress we could during the morning. So just after 0900 we slipped the mooring and headed out of Seaton Bay under sail. Within the hour we were becalmed.

Rather than waste fuel punching the tide we ghosted forwards in hot, hazy conditions with an almost glassy sea. Bearing in mind the anchoring difficulties of the previous evening I thought it a good time to add the 30 metres of rope I had bought some time ago at a boat jumble to the 20 metres of chain on board. The chain was more than enough in the Thames Estuary but was clearly not enough for these waters – I had not expected it to be. This was a long job which involved heaving up all the chain on deck and attaching the warp with an eye splice and shackle to the ring in the chain locker. When the job was done I just managed to drag all of the rope and then the chain back into the chain locker, which was now full to capacity. From now on when I weighed anchor I always had to go below and coax the final chain links down through the hawse pipe.

From time to time I scanned the horizon but like yesterday there were no other craft anywhere about. The morning had now gone and after lunch the tide turned in our favour but we were still becalmed so I started the motor. Our position was now something of a mystery – all I knew for sure was that we had been set offshore while I had been struggling with chain and rope down in the cabin, only mindful that we maintained reasonable sea room and were not on any collision course. I was glad to be back in the cockpit and at the helm on this hot summer's day. For about half an hour I had the surprising company of a racing pigeon, which landed on the cabin hatch and only flew off when I made to go below.

During the afternoon we passed Teignmouth and continued on in the direction of Torquay. We had been steering 240, and at 1615 we had a large pyramid of a rock on our misty starboard bow. I thought, hoped, it must be the Mewstone off Dartmouth, which I remembered from years ago. But it soon became clear that this was not the case – instead of the narrowing funnel into Dartmouth we had entered a broad concave bay. Our rock was in fact Hope's Nose off Torquay. On the far side of the very broad bay, Tor Bay, we made our way round the flat-topped red cliff of Berry Head and then poodled about looking for an anchorage for the night in Brixham Bay. A group of canoeists pointed out a favoured spot and confirmed where we were.

As I slowly moved up the learning curve I had to acknowledge that not only did I need to pay more attention to navigation but I also needed proper charts (my GPS was pretty useless without them), and an echo sounder.

Nevertheless, I reflected, as I enjoyed the warm, sunny, calm and picturesque evening, we were making progress.

The fine summer weather continued, making sailing out of the question. Between Brixham and Dartmouth we lost sight of land in poor visibility but there were several yachts and fishing boats about.

We passed outside the Mewstone off Dartmouth and continued on, seeing nothing more until at 1300 after three and a half hours steaming I muttered 'Land ho!' to myself a little uncertainly as I peered ahead. Fifteen minutes later we emerged from the mist to find ourselves a few cables off Start Point, whose diaphone was booming helpfully. Our arrival at Start Point was a veritable triumph of accidental navigation, for the tide had just turned in our favour. From this point, westwards to Plymouth and beyond, we would have a fair tide until about 1930.

As we motored towards Salcombe the mist cleared away, drenching us in glorious warm sunshine under a blue sky. Along the coast, red-brown cliffs alternated with the green valleys of Devon. This all had to be savoured not only for its own sake but also because this was now the furthest west I had ever sailed. In 1999 I had sailed as far as Salcombe to witness the total eclipse of the sun. There I had met up with my wife and family, who had travelled by road, and as a family we had pitched our folding caravan on the excellent vantage site of Prawle Point. We had seen a veritable tidal wave of cars surge into the tiny village in the morning and settle densely on the cliff tops like seabirds; we had seen several hundred boats come out of Salcombe and drop anchor just below us and we had seen the curtain of black velvet swiftly drawn across the land and seascape. Our breathless excitement had been tempered by the enchanting sight on the sea below us where all the little boats had switched their mast head lights on. Then the black velvet curtain was as swiftly drawn back and it was all over. Down below, the little boats dispersed unhurriedly, in contrast to the majority of motorists, who now took off in apparent impatience to join the inevitable traffic jams in the narrow country lanes. By tea time only a handful us, genuine holidaymakers, were left. All the day trippers had gone.

With mixed feelings, therefore – feelings of present pleasure, past nostalgia and lunchtime hunger – we hove-to off Bolt Head for cheese and pickle plus a lager and lime. It was all very agreeable.

During the afternoon we sailed and motor-sailed along the coast towards Plymouth. We came across another Mewstone – there seemed to be mewstones everywhere, no creek or inlet seemed to be complete without at least one. A glance at the chart showed this one to be off the entrance to the River Yealm at Wembury. 'That will do us nicely for the night,' I said to myself as I confirmed the situation by referring to the CA *Almanac*. Another yacht was obviously heading for the river, and I throttled back a little so that she could pilot us in, through the narrow entrance and over the bar. Once inside, we dropped the hook in deep water and delightful surroundings.

In the morning there was fog – not mist but really thick fog. Visibility was about a couple of boat lengths, no more. I expected it to lift as the sun rose higher, and it did, but it took its time. Before it dispersed completely boats started moving, several coming in from seaward. The skipper of one of these shouted something at me which I put together as he disappeared from view. I deduced that he was protesting that *Plover* was anchored just inside the channel. I checked. He was quite right and I was at fault. This had scarcely been obvious last evening when it was fine and when of course it didn't really matter anyway; but in the conditions of this morning's fog it was potentially dangerous.

6

Both sides of Cornwall

We did not need to leave the River Yealm until after midday, which gave me time to fix one or two things and give the boat a thorough spit and polish. We chose the safe way round into Plymouth Sound – in other words round the outside of the Great Mewstone, which is a very large off-lying rock, or small island, depending on your point of view.

I had no intention of stopping anywhere in Plymouth but it would have been ridiculous just to motor past the famous port without having a look. We had quite a fight against the tide to get inside the breakwater, which leaves an entrance or exit at either end. I took *Plover* the mile or so straight over to the Hoe, where I took photos of the famous Eddystone Lighthouse built by John Smeaton back in 1759 using dove-tailed blocks of stone for the first time. Then I unfurled the jib as we started to circle round Drake's Island, where Sir Francis anchored after his historic circumnavigation in 1580. Very soon though I had to furl it again as we headed towards Penlee Point and back out to sea.

By 1515 we were rounding Rame Head, from where we steered 280 in an almost flat calm. Our aim now was to reach Fowey, which port had been recommended to us.

With no real chart and the almost customary imperfect visibility I wrongly assumed that a busy trawler which hurried past us must be going into Fowey. We followed in her wake but lost her before we closed the shore, and finished up in what turned out to be Looe, some ten miles short of Fowey. I made a firm promise to buy charts either in Fowey or Falmouth.

We retreated from Looe only to be confronted by the Ranneys, a nasty collection of menacing rocks which we avoided by steering offshore and round the outside of the several boats fishing expectantly in their vicinity. Then we followed the line of the coast towards Fowey, being overtaken on the way by three other yachts.

The entrance to Fowey was well concealed and the harbour was very crowded. We meandered slowly through the closely moored pleasure boats, drinking in the picturesque attractions of the little port and enjoying the coloured sails of dinghies sailing sedately in the middle of the harbour.. Luckily we hit upon one of the visitors' pontoons, where there was just enough room for us right alongside the waste and recycling bins thoughtfully provided by the harbour authority.

A quick check on the fuel situation revealed that having motored all day with scarcely any sailing we had covered about thirty nautical miles and used eleven litres of fuel.

I fell in love with Fowey. The harbour itself is snug and there is always plenty of movement on the water. The little township is really quirky, with a single-carriageway main street running along the western side. There's a church and castle, both engineered into the hillside. Both overlook the Albert Quay, the focal point of the little township. The shops are all little traditional ones, with the national chains noticeably absent. No two houses seemed to be the same and almost all of them seemed to have at least one feature worth looking at, be it a bay window, painted doorway, hanging baskets, tiny courtyard, steps leading down to the water, overhanging gable, commemorative wall plaque or interesting name. It was all very charming and heart-warming.

I took the boat over to the Albert Quay for water and provisions. I also tried, unsuccessfully, to get the little Roberts clockwork radio fitted with an adaptor lead so that I didn't have to keep winding it up. This little radio gave surprisingly good reception, much better than the battery-operated one I also had on board. However having to wind it up every few minutes was a nuisance, and I would have liked to be able to plug it into the cigarette-lighter socket. Finally I bought an Admiralty folio of charts to get me round Land's End and as far as Hartland Point on the northern coast. Then I took *Plover* to a different visitors' pontoon for lunch

In the afternoon I used the water taxi to return to the Albert Quay and catch a bus to a point as near as possible to the Eden Project. The first part of the bus trip was especially interesting as the road zigzagged scenically up the hillside overlooking the picturesque harbour. Then followed a sample of the Cornish hinterland. Where the bus dropped me off left me with a three-mile hike in blazing weather to the famed Eden Project. It was worth the effort. I found the old quarry site a tasteful and imaginative engineering achievement.

I was surprised at the small number of visitors to the site, and I saw pretty well everything in the space of less than three hours, including of course the various biospheres and the innumerable garden plots; also the concert hall and amphitheatre. It must be quite memorable to attend a concert here. I was lucky to find an obliging bus driver in the car park who took me back to where I could get the St Austell service back to Fowey.

Back at the Albert Quay I enjoyed a portion of chips and can of drink before returning to the boat by water taxi.

In the next hour I had two visitors. First of all the garbage boat called at the pontoon and the crew enquired if the Avon pump and extensible aluminium paddles left on the pontoon nearby were mine. They had been there a couple of days apparently and were about to be binned. The pump did not look too good but the paddles were as good as new so I did the garbage boat crew a favour. When, a little later, the Harbourmaster drew alongside I showed him my receipt for the harbour dues I had paid in the morning but I think he had made the fees an excuse to have a chat. He was more interested in my little boat, over which he enthused at length despite its rather scruffy appearance. He was quite fascinated with our adventure so far. In return I learned from this friendly official that Fowey is still very much a working commercial port. The small freighters I had seen passing through the moorings were on their way to and from the wharf upriver, where they still load the china clay for which Cornwall became a famous source. Although the trade is now on a very much reduced scale, I was surprised to learn that it still existed at all. With other craft to attend to, the jovial Harbourmaster motored off – leaving me with a kindly print-out of the weather situation and forecast.

We left Fowey the following day after further unsuccessful attempts to get the wind-up radio and portable bilge pump repaired. Once clear of the harbour I hoisted sail and with a fair tide and the wind northerly 3–4 we sailed all afternoon all the way to the entrance to Falmouth harbour. This was by far our best sailing of the cruise so far and the only meaningful sail so far – that is to say the wind direction was exactly right for us to make progress strictly in the desired direction – a very rare experience.

During four hours of sailing the boat confirmed her dislike of being close-hauled and several times when I left the helm she gybed round in a full circle. More pleasingly we did catch up with one other yacht which really should not have happened – the crew must all have been asleep, drunk or dead! We used the engine to take us into St Mawes, opposite Falmouth, where I had a comical experience. In the crowded anchorage I selected an inshore buoy among the many smaller craft. Twice I just failed to pick up the favoured buoy with the boat hook and had to bear away and circle round other boats for another attempt. When I lined *Plover* up for a third approach I was astonished to find an obliging chappy in a rowing dinghy already on the mooring and holding up the riser, which he politely handed to me as I drew alongside! Whether he appreciated my difficulty and was just being genuinely helpful, or whether he had just tired of witnessing incompetence I don't really know!

We were now resolved to get round Land's End and into the Bristol Channel, and we were now within striking distance of achieving that unlikely ambition. We had the charts, the weather looked reasonable – all we needed was fuel. With this in mind we crossed the harbour first thing in the morning and tied up at the fuel berth of Falmouth Yacht Haven. There I was aghast to discover that they were charging £1.06 for a litre of unleaded petrol. I had refused to pay £1.00 a litre at Gosport but here I had no option. I just had to have full tanks for the next leg so I reluctantly handed over my credit card in return for 28 litres. Salt was then rubbed painfully into my wounded wallet when not many minutes after leaving the fuel berth at 0900 the engine cut out briefly.

The tide was due to turn against us at 0930 but ought to have little force so we ventured seawards towards the Lizard. It was warm and sunny with the wind still northerly and force 2. With all sail set we made steady progress over the ground. Half an hour after making a detour to avoid the menacing Manacle rocks we had the Lizard in view, and a couple of hours later we were rounding the famous promontory in calm conditions with scarcely any turbulence. We celebrated soon afterwards with a bite of lunch and a beer.

It took us three hours to cross Mount's Bay, all but twenty minutes without the engine. The wind was a brisk force 3 and for a while I reefed the jib. I had set my mind on anchoring for the night at St Michael's Mount and this we did at exactly 1800. We had the place to ourselves. This tidal island has been privately owned by the St Aubyn family for over three hundred years. It makes an unusual and quite striking anchorage but I was, in truth, a trifle disappointed, having visited its more famous French counterpart a few years previously. I was very pleased to be there, however. We had done quite well during the day, having covered 35 nautical miles in nine hours, most of it under sail. We were now poised for the outward mark.

Sunday 17 July was the twenty-eighth day of our adventure and therefore a good day on which to get round Land's End and turn for home, even if indirectly. Obviously we needed to work the tides correctly so that the last of the westward-flowing ebb carried us to the headland, after which the flood tide would whisk us into the Bristol Channel. The crucial time was 0945. I allowed two hours for the ten miles from St Michael's Mount, so at 0740 I coaxed the anchor chain down the hawse pipe and we set off in continuing glorious weather. The sea was a flat calm with no wind. The Inshore Waters forecast was variable 3 or less becoming west or southwest 3 or 4 – pretty well ideal! We raced along the coast, finding our new-found charts quite absorbing. No other craft could be seen in any direction so with the Tillerpilot behaving itself I washed and trimmed my hair and beard, both of which had become very long and scraggy, and then breakfasted. All that done, I felt really good. I could hardly believe that we had come so far.

By this time we were approaching Gwennap Head and our timing was absolutely 'spot on'. At 0950 I shouted 'Longships ahoy!' as our westernmost headland and off-lying rocks came into view. Excited and delighted, I decided to go round the outside of the Longships for photographic reasons. To this end I unfurled the jib and we motor-sailed until at 1030, with the rocks filling the viewfinder, I pulled the sail back round the forestay as we set course for the Brisons.

We passed inside the Brisons, a group of rocks and islets lying off Cape Cornwall, and made our way into the Bristol Channel. With the help of the flood tide we now made good progress over the ground and before midday we were off Pendeen Point, after which our course became more northeasterly. On the cliff tops derelict mine workings appeared, and I tried to snapshot them, but not very successfully.

We continued steadily along the Cornish coast, coming across no other craft until we turned into St Ives Bay. In St Ives harbour we picked up a buoy in order to have lunch. I then inflated the Redstart and rowed ashore. We needed drinking water, dry salt and batteries for the camera. This was a good opportunity to try out the aluminium paddles and pump left on the pontoon at Fowey by some forgetful boat owner. The pump was not much good but the paddles seemed a useful acquisition, though possibly a little weak.

After a purposeful fifteen minutes ashore I returned to *Plover* so as not to be trapped by the falling tide, which was going to leave the harbour completely dried out. With precious little water under the keels we scuttled out into the bay and dropped anchor among the fishing boats. I had no intention of moving further on that day – the tide was now a foul ebb and the next port would be distant Padstow. I spent the rest of the daylight hours doing checks, repairs and improvements around the boat. The state of the 12-volt batteries was beginning to cause me concern – they had not been recharged at all during the four weeks we had now been on passage.

7

The Bristol Channel

We sailed out of St Ives under the genoa, which was all the sail we needed. We were bound for Padstow, some 35 miles up the Bristol Channel. I reckoned we would have a fair tide from 1100 until 1800, which would help us on average less than half a knot. The forecast was of southwest winds 4–5 with rain at first, then showers. We started off in fine style, covering the ground smartly, and in two hours we reached the Medusa Rock off Newquay in a two-metre swell with quartering seas.

As we worked our way across Watergate Bay towards Trevose Head the seas built up and there was much white water as waves crashed heavily on the Quies Rocks, which I cautiously decided to go round on the outside. We could have gone inside, and the strong flood tide would no doubt have rushed us through the channel between the rocks and the mainland, but I knew that once committed we would have no chance of turning back. Taking the long way round was also a bit nerve-racking since the tide was all the time setting us strongly towards the rocks, so we had to crab our way to safety, tediously making sure that we moved forward at least as far as we drifted to leeward towards the rocks.

We had just about reached the position where we could begin to change course and let the tide whisk us into Padstow when to my great surprise a yacht appeared out of the murk ahead. She was crossing our bows and going fast and her course appeared to be set for Padstow. With relief we made to tuck in behind her to use her as a pilot. She was a knot or two faster than *Plover* and steadily drew away from us but at least we had a course we could confidently follow.

I now turned my thoughts to photography, with the lighthouse on Trevose Head and the menacing group of rocks marked on the chart as the Quies in mind. The swell was now in my estimation about three metres, with all horizons disappearing as the little boat slid down the quartering seas into quite dramatic troughs. I was reminded of the Stratos windsurfing adverts, the sensation of which we were sharing, in principle if not quite on that scale. I had just put the camera away and was thinking that really this was quite good fun when I was suddenly knocked flat as the stern of the boat was sheered sharply upwards. As I scrambled up I was horrified to see that the rudder had become unshipped and was balancing precariously under the pushpit right on the edge of the transom. With a nanosecond to spare I made a dash for it, grabbed it with both hands and hauled it inboard, the tiller still attached to the blade. My sweating and anxiety were by no means over, however, for until I had got the rudder back in commission, we were drifting at the mercy of the seas, with the possibility of broaching at right angles to the swell and in danger of filling with water. To slip the rudder onto its pintles is a precise and tricky enough job at rest in calm water. In the current situation it was not at all easy, but after much wiggling and balancing and a good deal of luck the job was done.

With the boat now, I thought, back under control I checked our position. We were still off Trevose Head and sea room was not an immediate problem although our pilot boat had disappeared. I tried to sheet in the genoa to resume cruising to Padstow, only to find that the starboard jib sheet was fouled, having become wrapped under the starboard bilge keel. This meant that the jib would not set properly, and with the tide now turned against us we found great difficulty in moving forward over the ground. With the unremitting swell still attacking us on the port quarter I dared not leave the helm to redeem the trapped rope, which was going to take a few minutes at best. Slowly, very slowly, the motor pushed us forward and gradually, very gradually, the sea state became less fierce. Finally I engaged the automatic steering and tackled the problem – first of all unknotting the jib sheet and then going forward to haul it back round the leading edge of the keel and finally back to the cockpit. Now we were back in command!

But our troubles were by no means over. We punched the tide, hugging the shore on our starboard side at a respectful distance. This led us into a wide bay, into which the swell continued to surge. I scoured the shoreline methodically clockwise, looking for a hidden channel which would lead us to Padstow, but there was no sign of any harbour or township, no boats, no jetties or pontoons, no trots of buoys, merely a few scattered dwellings and lots of relative nothingness. Far from finding anything, in fact I lost something, for the wind whipped off my head the rather smart yachting cap with a 'Wreck' motif which my ever-sceptical son, Conrad, had given me. I feared that the ebbing tide would soon dry out the whole of this bay, and with the rollers still sweeping into and across the bay I now looked for protection for the night. Accordingly we crossed the bay and found an excellent lee under the vertical cliffs of Stepper Point. There were a number of unwholesome-looking buoys jumbled on the surface with tangled slimy ropes only feet from the perpendicular rock face. The water was mercifully unruffled and, tested with the boathook, seemed deep enough to let us float all night. With sand appearing in every direction and the swell still pounding into the bay just a few boat lengths round the corner I thankfully tied *Plover* up, fore and aft, to a couple of the abandoned buoys, Her bowsprit was literally inches from the rock face. Mightily relieved, I wriggled out of my sailing togs and secured them to the boom to dry out. The cabin was in some disarray and while I set about straightening it out a shower of rain spitefully undid the drying-out of my jacket and trousers. After quite a day the kettle boiled, and I opened a few tins and unrolled my sleeping bag.

I slept soundly and the boat came to no harm during the night. The 0535 forecast was not good, however, and I felt it imperative to move from our present emergency mooring and get into Padstow, wherever that happened to be, before the wind got up. For some reason I thought this lay around the next headland and about three miles away. At 0620 we got under way, taking care not to get any of the slimy ropes round our prop. Against the tide we made slow progress and no entrance to Padstow appeared. Mystified, we continued along the coast until I had to realise that we were lost again!

With a now favourable tide we quickly made miles along the coast – but with the wind and sea state both mounting. Hartland Point became clear ahead, presenting me with a problem. That headland was as far as my folio of charts took me. Beyond there all I knew was that ports of refuge were few and far between. If we continued on round the point using the remaining flood tide we ought to get into the lee of the headland and hopefully to safety somewhere by nightfall. If we turned back towards a Padstow we had so far not been able to find, we would have a long hard slog against the tide and in conditions I would not knowingly have set out in.

I got the GPS working by changing its batteries, and found we were off Boscastle. I felt in need of advice so got on the VHF, paging the coastguards. I could not get through, receiving only squelchy discord. I tried and tried without success. Realising that I was not going to receive any advice, I was faced with the necessity of taking a decision. I erred on the side of the relatively known devil and set *Plover* on course to return towards Padstow.

Another unwelcome complication was that I was not too sure how long our fuel would last in these conditions. Anyway I started the outboard and began using it to gain sea room. Once safely offshore I would then cut the motor and use only the genoa for a long tack back along the coast. At intervals I continued to try to raise the coastguards but never successfully. I had not seen any other craft all day. Clearly we were in for a long tedious struggle back along the coast until the tide eventually turned in our favour. In the heavy swell the outboard was not at all happy, with the prop thrashing about with a fearful din when the stern was lifted almost clear of the water as seas passed under the boat. The motor also seemed to be loose on its bracket, though I could not see why.

In this state of resigned and complicated uncertainty you can imagine my amazement and joy when, in the middle of one of our motorised tacks offshore, I spied a mast and a bow wave surging over our port quarter – it was a lifeboat. I prepared to hail it but there was no need for it was plainly looking for us. The Padstow lifeboat hove-to and a member of the crew shouted across, 'Do you need any assistance?' I was a little uncertain how to respond for I had not asked them to come out and they might already be on a mission. 'I'm OK except that I am low on fuel – unleaded petrol, do you have any?' I replied. 'Yes we have, but we'll escort you back to Padstow,' came back the heartening reply. Thereupon I resumed heading offshore but after a few minutes standing by and watching the antics of the outboard, the lifeboat closed again and I was advised, 'We think it best if we take you in tow.' I did not argue – it would have been churlish to do so anyway, especially as they had obviously come out all this way on my behalf. In fact I was mightily pleased to accept their help. I don't think I could have borne it to see them just wave me farewell as they hurried back to port.

In the very bouncy conditions it took a few minutes for one of the lifeboat crew to jump aboard by little old tub. His name was James and his first job was to secure a tow line between the two boats – a line of incredible length. James then stayed on board with me while the RNLI towed *Plover* back the way we had come. This they did with extreme care, patience and consideration – very, very slowly so that there was never the slightest snatching of the tow rope and no possibility of any damage to my little craft. Consequently it took them five and a half hours, during which time James and I shared the cockpit, managing to talk most of the time. When James had answered the call he had only been home a few hours, having just returned after five days in the Irish Sea on a fishing boat. He told me that the Padstow lifeboat had so far had a very quiet year, and this was only their third callout.

In the cockpit it was cold and wet, from spray and rain squalls. When I went below briefly for some reason I immediately felt queer and back in the cockpit spewed over the side. James pointed out some of the notorious places along this inhospitable coast where various craft had come to grief – including the tragic old sailing boat *Maria Asumpta*, lost with several hands not so many years ago.

As we turned into Padstow Bay and calmer waters at the top of the tide I was astonished to notice that we were passing the very spot from which I had started that morning. It turned out Stepper Point, under whose cliffs we had spent the night, is where the River Camel flows into Padstow Bay, and is only about one mile from the harbour! If only I had known. I felt ashamed and guilty but James didn't utter a syllable of criticism as we were towed the final mile up the broad river which, when I had last seen it, was completely dried out and unrecognisable. James started the outboard and took us into the outer harbour, where he left me promptly to rejoin the rescue vessel – which then roared off downriver without delay to escape the falling tide. I didn't have time or opportunity to thank the coxswain and his crew. At that time I was unaware that Mike England, the lifeboat mechanic, had been taking photographs – and I am very grateful to him for allowing me to make use of some of them.

After arranging ropes and fenders I bailed out the cabin and re-stowed everything. My bedding and much of my clothing was soaked and what was not soaked was clammy. It was no place to spend the night, so I packed a rucksack and went ashore in search of bed and breakfast. At a hotel on the harbourside I was offered a room for £82 but I asked the lady receptionist if she knew of anywhere cheaper. She replied that she and her husband ran a bed and breakfast which would cost me £25 and was just five minutes up the hillside.

There I was made very welcome by the husband. I had a lovely hot shower before returning to the harbour to enjoy a relaxing meal in a restaurant instead of simply scoffing food from a chippy or takeaway. There I was able to linger over the food and wine while reliving the events of the day – cursing myself for my stupidity and counting myself very fortunate to have been rescued by the lifeboat. Back in my bedroom I was able to make myself a cup of tea before climbing into a large, clean, warm bed to watch a few minutes of TV before falling asleep. All's well that ends well ... (not completely well, however – I did have a sore coccyx, stiff back and sore throat as souvenirs of my day out in the Bristol Channel).

The day after my rescue was one of frantic varied activity. After a huge full English breakfast my landlady put me through to the RNLI, who had already been in touch – they wanted the basic information about me and my boat for their records. I also asked the coxswain to include my appreciation of their services and my heartfelt thanks. Before leaving my B&B I also spoke to a reporter from the Ipswich *Evening Star*, who phoned fortuitously via my wife; he seemed very interested in the trip so far and asked me to get in touch when I got the boat back home. I also had to square things at the Harbour Office, where the harbourmaster and his staff were most helpful. They thought it would probably be OK for me to leave the next day and they did their level best to help me do so. In the workshop they charged up my batteries and tried to repair my portable bilge pump and with their pick-up truck they filled up all my portable containers from the filling station on the outskirts of town. Next to the harbour office were coin-operated washing and tumble-drying facilities, which I used to the full. Most of the working day was in fact spent humping stuff from and to the boat, which was tied up in the outer harbour and a tidy hike from all the facilities. Luckily I was able to borrow a trolley from the harbour office which was a great help with the heavy batteries, water and fuel containers, bags of washing, etc.

The day passed quickly, and just in time I remembered that I desperately needed a chart of the Bristol Channel. I reached the chandlers as they were about to close and bought the only chart they had. I returned to the boat congratulating myself that I had made full use of all the helpful people and facilities of Padstow. I had enjoyed the busy day in the little Cornish port – I had landed among friends. As I pushed my trolley through the holidaymakers on the quays people smiled and asked how I was, members of the lifeboat crew introduced themselves and my landlord, who worked on the jetty with a megaphone drumming up passengers for trips up, down and across the river, made embarrassingly sure that they knew who I was and why I was there, always finishing with '... and he's 80 years old at that!'

All I had to do now was get the boat ready to sail in the morning. Poor old *Plover* was in a sorry state. Damp clothing was festooned from stem to stern, the cockpit floorboards were up, the rudder was off and I had to transfer fuel from five-litre containers to the main tanks, pump the bilges, fix the outboard bracket, check the Tillerpilot etc, etc. How I was going to get it all done so that I could leave in the morning I really did not know.

You can, therefore, imagine my amazement and delight when I was hailed in friendly fashion from the jetty. It turned out to be one of the lifeboat crew, Chris Murphy, who had made a point of coming along after his day's work to see how I was, have a chat, and make himself useful if he could. He ran a sizeable cycle hire business for a living, with a fleet of 200 machines. He had his young daughter with him, whom he promptly took home when he saw how much I had to do. He returned with some bolts I needed and then stayed with me until after dark, making a very businesslike job of fixing the outboard bracket and finding me a replacement electric bilge pump from his brother. He was a tremendous help and I felt flattered in the extreme that a lifeboatman should offer his services and friendship to the likes of myself. Without his help and skills I doubt whether I would have been able to move on next day. And his concern did not end there. When we had finished all the jobs on board Chris offered me a bed for the night, which I appreciatively declined, and we shook hands on the quayside. Then I remembered two things. Firstly I had a load of washing to collect from the harbour office and second I had missed out on shopping for provisions for the boat. The shops were now all long-since closed, of course. 'No matter, I can get by with what is on board,' I thought to myself. Imagine my surprise, therefore, as I was returning to the boat from the launderette when a car pulled up alongside. It was Chris again. He had been home, made some sandwiches and packed up some fruit for me for the next day! I still cannot think what I had done to deserve such friendship and consideration.

On my way to collect my late-night laundry I had a word with a couple of yacht crews who I understood were locking out in the morning. They surprised me by saying that the weather forecast had been downgraded and they were not now going. This left me thinking that I was going to be in Padstow for at least one more day. I was surprised therefore when I heard the 0535 forecast which was not unreasonable – winds northwesterly 3–4 becoming variable – and slid back the hatch, to see that the lock gates were already open and the inner harbour was emptying as yachts motored out.

I decided to scud round to the harbour office for the local forecast. This agreed with the BBC forecast and I noticed that the two yachts had already sailed. I decided to do likewise, hurried back to the boat and cast off at 0640. In the estuary the wind was against the tide, making things a little lumpy. I was hoping to get as far as Lundy by nightfall and could only do this with the help of a fair tide, which was not due until just after noon and would then be in our favour for about six and a half hours, hopefully giving the winds time to moderate. Bashing against the ebb from breakfast time until midday seemed pointless and would probably move us forward at most ten miles, so I looked for deep water in the estuary in which to anchor.

An hour before low water the ebb was running much

less powerfully so I hauled up the CQR and we motored seawards and set course for Hartland Point. Once clear of Padstow Bay the tide turned in our favour and we made good headway along the coast in bouncy conditions with an overcast brisk breeze treating us to occasional bright periods. We motor-sailed, the jib giving us an extra knot or so besides steadying the boat. It was 1700 when we sighted Lundy, dim, small and distant on the blurred horizon. Clearly we were not going to reach the island on this flood tide so we deliberately steered up-channel in order that the ebb, when it commenced, would drift us back seawards as we steered across the stream. Our devious course to the island could not avoid our crossing the shipping lane to the ports of South Wales and Avonmouth and we did in fact have to keep an eye on a couple of inward-bound ships, the first ships I had seen since leaving Fowey.

Around 1930 the effect of the ebb became appreciable and I furled the jib. The clouds cleared away and I was able to enjoy steering towards the setting sun with the island gradually looming larger on our port hand. It took an hour and a half to reach the anchorage under the southeast prominence of Lundy, where about a dozen yachts and fishing boats were riding at anchor. The tidal range here in the middle of the Bristol Channel is considerable and as the Bidata was 'on the blink' I asked a couple of skippers how much chain they had out and got wildly differing answers – ten metres and forty metres! We were just two days short of spring tides but I succeeded in getting a hold after paying out all of our thirty metres of chain and five metres of our new rope for the first time. It was not enough, however, for at 0230 I had to turn out as we were getting rather too friendly with a large fishing boat. As I started our motor and hauled up the anchor I noticed that another yacht nearby was doing the same.

After my recent struggles it would have been wonderful

to spend a couple of days relaxing on this celebrated island, enjoying the bird life and the flora. Like many people I had often dreamed of a holiday with the Landmark Trust on this nature reserve – quite an expensive one when one adds the boat fares from the mainland to the accommodation costs. Yet here I was, after an admittedly uncomfortable and disappointing night, preparing to leave without even setting foot on this tiny gem – it measures only two and a half miles by less than a mile wide, with granite cliffs soaring up to 120 metres. I resisted the temptation, however, because I was anxious to reach the relative safety of the South Wales coast before the weather deteriorated. But I had to be very mindful of the notoriously powerful tides of the Bristol Channel. I needed their friendship and could not afford to oppose them. According to the pilot book, 'Lundy Island is surrounded by tidal races and overfalls and should only be approached near slack water. Tidal streams run typically between two and four knots but at the Severn Bridge up to 6 knots.' I worked out that if we got under way at 1240, round about the turn of the tide, we could have up to eight hours of flood tide running at an average of 2.5 knots, which should allow us to get to Swansea by nightfall.

Actually we upped anchor just before one o'clock, the 32 metres of chain and warp taking more than ten minutes to coax into the chain locker, the final links having to be hauled down through the hawse pipe from the cabin below. We left Lundy with dry bilges, most of my clothes were dry-ish, and we had about 52 litres of fuel on board. The weather was calm, warm and sunny with moderate visibility. Our course was 020 and our target was the Worms Head on the Gower Peninsula.

In less than two hours the Welsh coast was visible through the murk ahead. There was no wind and it was warm, with no other craft in any direction. At 1640 the

Worms Head was clear ahead and we changed course to 060, on which we would gradually close the coast en route for the Mumbles. A ferry from Cork to Swansea hurried out of the haze astern, swept past us and vanished around Mumbles Head.

As evening unfolded it became clear we would be lucky to reach Swansea, and after a glance at the chart I decided to anchor for the night in the calm conditions. We could go into Swansea in the morning if we wanted to – for fuel and provisions. A beautiful little bay, more a cove, opened up. This was, I reckoned, the location of Mumbles village, and I spent a while trying to reconcile the chart with the CA handbook, which listed an anchorage north of Mumbles Pier. I could not see any pier (it was in fact a couple of miles further on round the Mumbles Head), but I was delighted with the little cove and contentedly dropped the hook. I phoned lifeboatman Chris Murphy in Padstow, who was pleased that we had made it to Wales.

I was enjoying my evening meal when I was mystified by a loud hissing-cum-roaring sound, so I poked my head out of the hatch. To my astonishment I found that we were about to take the ground in the middle of a bay that was rapidly drying out. The surf breaking on a sand bar was the source of the sound, and in no time we were high and dry on firm golden sand. I had not bargained on this but it didn't matter. It did serve to remind me, however, not only of the strength of the tides hereabouts but also of their enormous range. I resolved to be on watch when we refloated in the morning.

While I was listening to the early-morning shipping forecast a man walking his dog gave a friendly knock on the hull with his stick and wished us 'Good morning'. At that time ships of the desert would have been more at home in our little cove than real ships. But half an hour later we were afloat – another reminder of the forces at play in the lively Bristol Channel. The tide started surging into the bay at 0545, and twenty minutes later *Plover* was bumping uncertainly on the sandy bottom. Ten minutes later we were properly afloat in rapidly deepening water. I washed and breakfasted before getting the anchor up about half past seven.

We motored out of the little bay bound for Swansea and needing drinking water, provisions and possibly fuel. Conditions were currently calm, though we had to punch the tide. The forecast, however, was not at all good. Sole and Lundy sea areas were to expect cyclonic winds force 4–5 with squalls developing later in the west, force 6–7. For inshore waters the forecast was variable 3–4 becoming southeast later on.

As we approached Mumbles Head I spied the missing pier with the little township and a multitude of various craft moored and at anchor. I decided to join them and push on when the tide slackened off – it seemed a pointless waste of time, fuel and opportunity struggling into Swansea just to come out again. It was nine o'clock when we moored up. Twice I failed to pick up a buoy in the fast-running tide and an attempt to anchor was not successful. Again I selected a buoy, this time successfully, though nearly disastrously, for I slipped on the foredeck and very nearly finished up as a man overboard. My Help the Aged deck shoes from Gosport were responsible, and from then on I went back to my old trainers. As I sipped a cup of tea I reflected on the exciting life I was leading – it was now 0930 and already, since reveille, I had witnessed the power and behaviour of the channel tides, had motored along the coast round the Mumbles and narrowly escaped a dunking. What next, I wondered?

And well I might – for more surprises and excitement were in store. While waiting for the tide I bailed a bucket and a half from the cabin bilge and found that several nuts on the outboard bracket were vibrating loose. I tightened them all up, with the result that it was now impossible to raise the bracket when the motor was not needed. That was not ideal, for all the time the motor was in the water its sacrificial anode was eroding rapidly away in the salt water. We now had thirty litres of petrol on board.

At 1320 we got under way, when the hire craft whose buoy we had picked up returned to claim his mooring. We set off on a course of 135 after the compass settled down after a fit of wild swings – which seemingly were cured when I opened the throttle! As we crossed the buoyed channel into Swansea the tide was no longer serious and it was mild, calm and warm with force 1 on the nose and moderate visibility.

The lack of an echo sounder was a constant frustration and it caused a period of low-level anxiety as we closed the eastern side of Swansea Bay, where a group of drying banks lay right in our path. Some of these were made conspicuous by breaking water. Once past that hazard a more serious problem arose. The weather was rapidly deteriorating, the wind rising and the sea state becoming more turbulent. Off Porthcawl things became distinctly lumpy and, bearing in mind the poor weather forecast and my recent experiences off the Cornish coast, I thought it wise to seek shelter. But there was none. I passed the comically named Fairy Buoy and then had a close look at Porthcawl Harbour, which was totally dry, for the flood tide was still very young. Turning back against this tide was unappealing, leaving the only option to continue. I put to sea again and got into my Henri Lloyds. As I was struggling to get the hood over my head I caught a movement out of the corner of my eye. I was absolutely astonished to find an RNLI inshore lifeboat not a boat's length away on our port side with its crew looking very businesslike and impressive. After enquiring if I was OK the coxswain asked if I was aware that there was a strong winds warning in force for the Bristol Channel with easterly winds force 6 expected within the next twelve hours. Of course I was not aware – though I had not forgotten the early-morning shipping forecast, which had been buoyant enough. After a few moments' thought I told the lifeboatmen that I felt my best course was to carry on to Cardiff – I was doing an estimated five knots at least over the ground, which would get me to Cardiff in about three hours and hopefully before things got really nasty. The Cox'n agreed after making sure that we had VHF and a mobile phone on board. Then they were off in a frothy flurry of white water.

How and why the inshore lifeboat had buttonholed us made me wonder. Perhaps they were patrolling to warn all craft navigating their patch, possibly they were just on a routine training exercise, or maybe they had been warned by the Padstow people that *Plover* was heading up-channel towards Bristol. Anyway, whatever the reason, I was grateful for their visit.

We steered outside the weighty prominence of the Tusker Rock with its white collar of breaking water and then along the gloomy overcast coast towards Nash Point, about five miles ahead. Again I regretted that I had no depth sounder. There were two ways to get round this headland – either steer outside everything, thus venturing into the worst of wind-against-tide conditions, or risk the inshore channel between the headland and the off-lying Nash Sand. The sandbank is about three miles long, dries over three metres and gradually converges on the Point, creating a funnel into which the flood tide naturally speeds up into a race. Once into the funnel there could be no turning back for a little boat like *Plover* with her 5-horsepower engine. Nevertheless the inshore option seemed to be the lesser of the two evils. Visibility was not good but the cliffs of the coast were clear enough and so too became the surf which was breaking increasingly close on the long sandbank on our starboard side. At the end of the funnel there is an east cardinal buoy, which was helpful, as the channel narrows to a width of only about two hundred yards. Spring tides are here reputed to flow at a healthy five knots around the times of new moon and full moon. Hand-steering, we fairly surged though the channel, under the lighthouse and past the buoy. On our left-hand side a rocky mainland ledge menaced angrily while just as near on our right-hand side turbulent white water was kicking up ferociously on the sand bank. We emerged, heart pumping furiously, from the funnel and into the turbulence which is normally found around headlands. This did not last for long, and once through that I breathed a mighty sigh of relief.

An interesting and eventful day was by no means over, however. An hour or so later, off Breaksea Point with its modern power station, the outboard suddenly cut out. Although I managed to restart it, the motor played up all the way, running for less and less time before stopping. Cardiff was now out of the question, and I began to think we would be lucky to make Barry, which we were approaching under jib alone. The entrance to that port was well concealed, and in searching for it we were in danger of going aground on a lee shore. Just in time I put the boat about and hastily hauled up the mainsail to get us vital sea room. The entrance to Barry was fortuitously revealed when a large tanker, anchored in the roads, weighed anchor and slowly made her way inshore towards the still-hidden way in to the port. We had to be careful not to get swept by the tide past the entrance, while avoiding getting in the way of the tanker. The latter proved to be the easier, for with a now very light wind but a vigorous tide we had to fight for every inch as we crabbed our way across and against the tide towards the jetties of the outer harbour. By dint of tense helming, and with my heart in my mouth, we just managed to slide into the safety of the harbour. There I got the sails down and then used my canoe paddle to get to a mooring. I always carry this long-handled paddle on board to provide the propulsion of last resort. When engines and sails fail it is still possible to manoeuvre the boat to some degree using this device, and there have been several occasions when I have been thankful to have it clipped on deck. This was the first time I had used it on this trip, and it enabled us to juggle with the complexities of mooring up fore and aft between two buoys, in common with all the other craft in the harbour. Later a helpful couple sailing a dinghy came over and put me in the picture regarding the harbour, the yacht club and the locality – in return for details of my trip so far. When at last I was able to flop into the cabin and put the kettle on, I felt that I had certainly earned my grub this day. Unfortunately we had very little of this on board – no bread, no butter, no cheese and no wine, and we were out of biscuits and cakes, with no marmalade or basic meals. I scratched together a hash of corned beef and marrowfat peas – the leftovers from which I had for breakfast next morning.

Barry harbour dries out completely to a mucky, muddy bottom, as I was able to confirm when I was awakened at half past two in the morning. The predicted force 6 I had been warned about by the RNLI was now howling through the rigging and drips from the forward hatch were wetting my clothing bag below. I moved the bag and placed saucepans strategically to catch the drips before returning to my sleepsack. I modified my language when I thought what it must be like out in the Bristol Channel. How glad I was not to have succumbed to the temptations of the island of Lundy!

After my unconventional breakfast I inflated the Redstart and rowed ashore to the Yacht Club, where I was made very welcome. The clubhouse is very well appointed, with a wonderful view over the harbour and the two islands in the middle of the Bristol Channel, Steep Holm and Flat Holm, which names aptly describe their relative profiles. Customarily members can enjoy a full traditional roast lunch in the bar/dining room on Sundays. Happily, by chance, it was a Sunday and I was anxious not to miss such a treat. I booked a meal but first needed to do essential shopping at the local shops, one of which was hopeless, the other very well stocked. With several heavy plastic bags I sweated it back to the clubhouse, where they had kindly kept a lunch back for me. It was delicious, and enormous. Members were very friendly and interested in my experiences. After lunch I enjoyed a hot shower and then returned to the bar to chat with members and ultimately stretch out and have forty winks.

When *Plover* refloated in the early evening I went back on board to cover the forward hatch and rig up the boom cover and get the boat better organised. Rudi Graham phoned from Ipswich to congratulate me on reaching Wales and I surprised my table tennis team mate, Barrie Hart, by phoning him from Barry – he was suitably astonished. I had now been *en voyage* for five weeks.

We were now only thirty miles from Bristol and the inland waterways system, where the weather would no longer be a serious factor and daily progress would be a near certainty. But it was to be another whole week before I was able to continue. Easterly winds were now disappointingly forecast for the next few days. However, I had much to do on board – first and foremost to sort out the outboard motor. I had a go at this after first rowing ashore with my fuel cans, water container and bags of rubbish. Rachel, who ran the adjacent boatyard with her husband David, drove me to the nearest filling station, fully three miles away, and I was able to add 17 litres to the onboard supply. I filled up the integral fuel tank on the

Mariner outboard but this did not make a scrap of difference to its performance – it still kept cutting out after running for a few seconds. After lunch I rowed ashore again – this time to visit Cardiff. But first I needed help with the outboard. Rachel recruited a young yard worker who was willing to come out to the boat after working hours. We agreed to meet at the yard at seven o'clock, by which time the boat should be ready to refloat.

I was now free to jump on a train to Cardiff for a very reasonable £2.30 return. From the station I explored the centre of the city and then hiked off in the direction of Cardiff Bay. Here the massive redevelopment of the old notorious Tiger Bay was not yet complete but it was already impressive, with striking architecture around Mermaid Quay and the Millennium Centre. Nobody could tell me what the Welsh wording on the frontage of the latter meant! The Welsh Parliament building will, I suppose, more or less complete the upgrading of the area, which, with its wide open spaces, needs quite a lot of people and activity to bring it to life. In the bay itself nothing was going on and at the pontoons a mere handful of yachts and small craft were tied up.

I shopped cheaply at Iceland and returned to Barry to meet up with Royston. He stripped down and cleaned the carburettor of the Mariner and made minor adjustments but really found nothing wrong. Nevertheless when he had finished it all seemed to be fine. After rowing the young mechanic ashore I took the boat over to the other side of the harbour, where there was water deep enough for the lifeboat. We rafted up alongside three magnificent traditional Bristol Pilot Cutters. As I was putting springs out, the crew of one of them returned. They were friendly and helpful but explained that they intended leaving at 0500 in the morning. Accordingly I set my alarm for 0400.

Before leaving harbour the skipper of the Bristol Pilot

Cutter made a point of having a word about the last thirty miles of the Bristol Channel. Bristol was his home port and he obligingly spread his large-scale chart on deck and systematically went through all the hazards between Barry and Avonmouth. It all sounded offputtingly horrendous, culminating with a seemingly almost impossible exit from the Bristol Channel into the River Avon. Not only was this hard to find but it needed to be made before the ebb flowing out of the river made it both difficult and unwise. It made me wish that I could borrow this large-scale chart, that I had an echo sounder, that I had a crew and that I had a more powerful engine and a less powerful weather forecast. To complete the total destruction of my confidence the 0535 forecast was for northeast winds force 3–5 increasing to 5 later. They would be right on the nose and opposing the tide. What could be nicer?

As I waved farewell to the classic boat I noted that there was already an uncommon amount of wind for so early an hour in the morning. After my recent briefing I scarcely needed an excuse for not leaving port, and I decided not to leave harbour – discretion for once triumphing over valour to put a kindly gloss on things. After breakfast I moved the boat back across the harbour once again, needing help from a couple of club members to secure her fore and aft and head to wind.

I did not leave the boat all day, finding plenty to do on board – getting the new bilge pump to work, bailing the cabin bilge, cleaning and drying out the sail locker and using Life Caulk to tackle leaks through the cabin roof. I also rigged the heavy-duty boom cover over the cockpit – for heavy rain was forecast for the night and the morrow. I also unshipped the rudder as a precaution. In the evening Margot read me over the phone an article which had been published in the Ipswich *Evening Star*, and we discussed our forthcoming joint anniversary celebrations.

Next morning the cabin was dry but the forecast on a grim-looking morning was similar but worse, with headwinds up to force 6 in a murky crystal ball. Then at 1305 the coastguards broadcast a Severe Weather Warning for Lundy and the Bristol Channel with little improvement before Sunday! I pumped up the Avon to row ashore for some shopping but it started pouring with rain and I spent a second day on the boat. After topping up my phone card I rang my in-laws Les and Audrey at Monmouth. From them I received an almost ecstatic welcome, with an offer to come down immediately to collect me. That really wasn't practical, since the boat would be on the mud until after dark, so we agreed I should abandon ship in the morning. I spent two most enjoyable and civilised days at Monmouth. Audrey cooked some cordon bleu meals, I luxuriated for a couple of hours in the bath (not realising that the only toilet in the house was in the bathroom), and Audrey made a couple of plastic bags of my much-worn clothing wearable again. In return I was happy to be able to help Les do some heavy pruning on an out-of-hand sycamore tree in the back garden. On Sunday afternoon, 31 July, I was returned to *Plover* with mixed feelings. My refresher course on the benefits of civilisation – its comfort, space, colour and warmth, the attractions of hot water, companionship and good food – had been a real tonic.

Back at Barry Yacht Club, Les helped me recover the inflatable from the lock-up shed and get it down the slipway and loaded up. Then I said '*au revoir* and thanks' to Les and Audrey, who had almost turned the bad weather into a blessing in disguise.

Back on board, I moved *Plover* into deep water near the lifeboat, ready for departure in the morning, and thus concluded my sixth week on passage. The hold-up due to bad weather had been extremely frustrating. At Barry we were only thirty miles from Bristol and once there we would be unworried by tides and the weather for we would be on inland waterways. I was now a man in a hurry, for in less than four weeks Margot and I were throwing the biggest party of our lives in celebration of our eightieth birthdays. Margot was bearing the brunt of the preparations and needed help. With each passing day I felt more guilty. In the event of any more mishaps or delays I was prepared to leave the boat in care somewhere and go home by train, returning to *Plover* after the celebrations were all over. I really had to get to Bristol without further delay.

The forecast was quite good, and when we motored out of Barry harbour at 0900 into the Bristol Channel there was very little wind and it was calm, grey and overcast but mild. By 1015 we had passed Flatholm and Steepholm and reached the Monkstone Lighthouse, which sticks up prominently out of the middle of the channel.

From the lighthouse I was for a time uncertain of our proper course. I steered 060 after reference to the chart but failed to pick up the buoys marking the safe water to Avonmouth. The Bristol Channel was still about ten miles wide and I could see both the English and Welsh coasts. When I located the pier of Weston-super-Mare I was reassured and the Magellan confirmed our position.

My next concern was the engine, which suffered a series of sudden cut-outs. Each time she restarted promptly but I could not afford for this to continue, much less get worse. I could see bubbles in the fuel filter and wondered how air might be getting into the system. I had made it a practice to run on both thirty-litre tanks simultaneously and it occurred to me that maybe this was something to do with it. I shut off the starboard tank. There was one more stoppage and then no more.

We chugged up the Severn Estuary between the buoys and I referred to the chart and the CA *Almanac* regarding the easy-to-miss confluence of the River Avon. A small coaster overtook us off Portishead and I hoped she might give us a pointer or two. Rain threatened so I dived below for my heavy-weather gear. As I zipped up the trousers we passed a red can buoy which I identified as the Cockburn. 'The Cockburn ... my God! Hell's bells, we're here already!' I exclaimed to myself. 'Steer 098 for the entrance immediately south of the south pier of Avonmouth docks,' was what the almanac advised, and I had taken the precaution of memorising the directions. I swung the tiller onto the new course. This took us to a severe-looking jetty with a square brick tower overlooking a small bay. There was no obvious inlet from the landward side.

We did a slow circle but there were no helpful buoys, arrows or other markers to be seen. Mystified, I repeated to myself the entrance directions. 'Immediately south' really must mean immediately, I concluded, so we went over to the jetty which we then closely followed inshore – unconfidently hoping that a river entrance would open up. One did! It was unobtrusive, it was narrow, it was calm and its sides were very muddy. But it was the River Avon, the all-important River Avon, the Rubicon, Mount Everest and Cape Horn of my little trip. I began to wonder why I was so much more excited by this unlikely and unprepossessing rendezvous than I had been by Land's End. I surmised that at the Longships the sun was shining and with the length of the Bristol Channel still ahead the overall success of the project was still very much in doubt. Here, although it was a bit gloomy, with a long leg of inland waterways now ahead, I felt that the circumnavigation would almost certainly be completed.

The flood tide now gently carried us the six twisting miles to Bristol between high banks of black mud. As we got near to the city I began to peer round each bend of the river, looking for my first glimpse of the Clifton suspension bridge. It had been an ambition of mine for years to sail under this famous landmark, and as we approached and passed under it I became quite trigger-happy with the digital camera.

Upstream of the bridge lies the lock, from which a day-trip pleasure boat fortuitously emerged. As it passed us with several friendly waves a bright green light appeared high on the lockside. We entered the huge lock with our longest ropes coiled on deck fore and aft and followed the lock-keeper's instructions. I had been wondering how I would be able to control the boat as the lock filled but I need not have worried. As we came to a halt beneath the massive dripping and slimy wall the lock-keeper lowered a coil of heaving line down to us, which he would then have hauled back up after I had attached our own rope. However I had spotted a ladder midway along the lock wall and preferred to control our rise from tidal to non-tidal waters from there using just a short breast rope slipped through the rungs. We locked through entirely on our own, using goodness knows how many gallons of water. The massive gates of this very large lock create considerable turbulence as they open and close, and I had overlooked this, so we were swung about quite surprisingly when we tried to help the lock-keeper by making a prompt exit.

A swing bridge operates in time with the lock gates, and once beyond that we were into the Floating Harbour. I had spent several days there in 1996 and remembered it well. There were changes, of course. Many buildings and properties overlooking the water had been spruced up, and some were now brightly coloured. There were many more pleasure and commercial craft in great variety at pontoons and wharves on both sides. The SS *Great Britain*, Isambard Brunel's masterpiece, freshly painted, looked absolutely stunning. The forethought, expense, planning, engineering and seamanship involved in bringing this historic vessel back to her home port from the Falkland Islands must surely have been worth the effort, and as we passed slowly by I murmured a little 'thank you' to all those who made a contribution in whatever form. Just under the stern of the mighty steamship the replica of John Cabot's *Matthew* has been found a home. We had seen her nearly ten years ago, just before she made her commemorative voyage across the Atlantic to Newfoundland. Both achievements, the original voyage of discovery and that of the replica, defy belief.

8

The Kennet and Avon Canal

I found a mooring for *Plover* opposite the Industrial Museum and the Arnolfini. This turned out to be a long-stay, secure pontoon and therefore equipped with both water and electrical points, and I wasted no time in plugging in the trickle charger to give the ship's batteries a much-needed boost. I was lucky, for the previous occupant had left £1.32 in credit (by morning the no. 2 battery was fully charged at a cost of 7 pence). I phoned Margot, who was amazed at our progress, and then Les and Audrey, who were likewise impressed. I, too, was pleased and uncorked a bottle of red wine to go with my cheese and pickle lunch. After forty winks I began to prepare the boat for the inland waterways leg of the journey by getting the sails, boom and running rigging all off the boat, ready for lowering the mast next day. A fuel check showed we had 27 litres still on board. We had now been six weeks on passage.

We left the pontoon after lunch next day and meandered slowly down the harbour looking for likely places where I could get the mast down. Nowhere seemed ideal and I finished up at the Harbour Office, where I had to pay my dues (£5 for 24 hours). There I was able to tie up to a visitors' pontoon where there was ample space and also stability. In the workshop I had no difficulty recruiting a couple of able-bodied workers to help me drop the mast, which only took a few minutes. The staff in the office were very helpful, printing out for me the several pages of a complete map of the waterway from Bristol to Reading. They also told me that the next opening of the Redcliffe Bridge, which barred our exit from the Floating Harbour and our arrival in inland waterways proper, would be at 1615, and I resolved to go through at that time. That should have given me time enough for a lunch in the hot sunshine of the cockpit and then time enough to lash down and tidy up all the rigging. In fact we cut things very fine indeed, arriving off the swing bridge seconds after 1615. Despite my gesticulations the lock-keeper refused to open the bridge and waved us back. I studied the bridge, however, and decided we could probably sneak under it – which we did with an inch or two to spare and much to the chagrin of our learned friend.

We were now free to make haste out of Bristol and we made a good start, finding the lock open at both ends at Netham where we re-joined the tidal River Avon. This lock only becomes necessary when the tide in the river exceeds 32 feet – and that is some eight miles upstream from Avonmouth! Our next lock was at Hanham, where we were due to leave the tideway for the last time and enter the canalised river. Between the two locks of Netham and Hanham we passed through lonely, steeply wooded and attractive countryside with few buildings and fewer boats. It was all so very green, picturesque, calm, peaceful and innocuous in contrast to the often grey, stormy, threatening and inhospitable Bristol Channel which we had just left.

At Hanham Lock, where the Kennet and Avon Canal begins, there was bad news and good news. First of all I discovered that I did not have a lock handle on board. I had obviously forgotten to stow one before leaving home, where I had two. This meant I would have to purchase a third to add to my growing collection. Then, when I presented myself at the lock-keeper's cottage, I learned from the not very efficient locum that the fulltime official was on holiday and while that was so, boats had a free passage through the canal. This was good news indeed – if one had a lock handle. Unfortunately the deputy keeper only had one of these and she was therefore unable to lend, give or sell me one. I would have to wait until the morning and get one from the nearby marina. However her young daughter, bless her, did her best to make amends by using the one existing handle to help me through the lock, which nevertheless filled pitifully slowly although the rise was only a couple of feet. In moderately heavy rain we continued as far as Keynsham, where the next lock brought our travelling for the day to an indisputable end.

Once I had obtained a lock handle, at a cost of £12, from the marina chandlery, we were able to work our way through Keynsham lock. There are 105 locks between Hanham and Reading, and at No. 5 we came across our first difficult one. This was at Kelston, traditional home of Fry's chocolate. Here British Waterways staff were changing the gearing on the paddles, making them easier to raise but also making it easier for the windlass to work its way off the spindle. They offered no help in working the lock, however, and when they had done their job they scuttled off – presumably for their lunch. Because the bottom gate was leaking a level either side could not be reached and I was quite unable to get *Plover* out of the lock. In the end I just had to wait until a narrowboat came along to provide the extra muscle needed to force open the gates.

At Bath I was in two minds. On the one hand I hoped to have a lunch break in the very heart of the city by the horseshoe weir and under the unique and historic Pulteney

◀ First sight of the Clifton Suspension bridge

▶ SS *Great Britain*

◀ Before the mast comes down in Bristol

► The greens of the
Avon valley

▲ Working the
Caen Hill flight

► Leaving the
Bruce Tunnel

◀ Ready to
lock out

▲ Hungerford

◀ Riverside
gathering

▲ Cruising in company with *Four Miles On*

◀ Limehouse Basin: back in sailing mode

▶ The last mile

Bridge. On the other hand I wanted to get clear of the Widcombe flight of locks as soon as possible. My mind was made up when I saw several boats tied up at the entrance to the bottom lock. I thought it wise to get into the queue straight away; lunch could wait. Actually we did not have long to wait, and *Plover* was able to squeeze into the Widcombe lock with a couple of narrowboats, one longer than the other. The longer boat filled the right-hand side of the lock, leaving the left-hand side to the shorter narrowboat in front and *Plover* behind. In this formation we worked our way up the six locks of the flight. There used to be seven locks but a road improvement scheme involved the combining of two of them. This created the Bath Deep Lock, which moves boats up or down nearly twenty feet at a time and is one of the deepest in the country.

From the top lock we had a very slow passage to Bathampton trailing a narrowboat which we could not overtake. There is a speed limit of four miles per hour on the canals and narrowboats in particular are very good at respecting this. They are also very scrupulous about reducing speed when passing moored craft. The speed limit is imposed in order to minimise damage to the banks by the wash which long and heavy narrowboats, in particular, could create if travelling at higher speed. Little *Plover*, however, with her light displacement, can travel much faster without creating a serious wash. As I was now in a hurry we tended to exceed the speed limit whenever it was possible to do so without causing erosion of the banks or annoyance to other canal users.

At Bathampton the waterside George Inn is an attractive and obviously popular spot with both boating and motor-car travellers, and we stopped there for a belated lunch. But my hopes of enjoying a lager with my usual cheese and pickle were confounded by the crazy situation at the crowded bar where one poor girl was trying to cater for a room full of thirsty customers. After a few pointless minutes waiting in the queue I walked back to the boat and had a swig of wine instead.

From Bathampton to Bradford-on-Avon we enjoyed the steep wooded Avon valley with its two small aqueducts. Very few boats were moving but along the made-up towpath cyclists, hikers and joggers were making good use of the Avon Walkway. At Bradford we moored up for the night at the Canal Tavern just below the lock. There I did have a lager, though I was too late for bar food and had to eat on board. During the day we had managed twelve locks and two swing bridges. We had 21 litres of fuel still in the tanks.

We got under way with a flurry of excitement in the morning, which was a really lovely one. As soon as respectable I grabbed the camera and fuel trolley and breezed off to the filling station, which was only a few minutes' walk away. I bought 13.5 litres and then went off on a brief photo safari. The old mill town, which is built on both sides of the River Avon and canal, mostly out of mellow Bath stone, has great charm. In the middle of the medieval nine-arched stone bridge is a tiny chapel which apparently served for a time as the local jail. The cricket field was a picture.

Next I hiked off to the local supermarket to stock up with food and drink. As I returned to the boat I noticed that the lock was being worked – in our favour. Ever the opportunist, I dashed across the bridge and back to the mooring, where I unceremoniously threw the shopping into the cabin, cleared the cockpit, started the engine and cast off the ropes. The lock was only a few boat lengths away so I shouted and gesticulated at the guys working the paddles to hold everything. Mercifully they heard me, re-opened the gates and made way for *Plover*. Above the lock we pulled in to the water point, where we filled up with drinking water and had a late breakfast.

We had an easy start to the day, with no locks for the first five miles. At Semington there are two locks, which we shared with the N/B *Grigory*. Two miles further on we were joined for the ascent of the Seend flight of five locks by a motor cruiser, *Indaloo*, crewed competently by a young couple. As a single-hander I was spared the hard work of working the locks. All I had to do, while the other boat crews wound the paddles up and down and pushed the gates open and closed, was to stay on the boat and manoeuvre her in and out. Nevertheless poor *Plover* was taking a bashing in the miniature locks of this toy system of inland waterways. She had already lost some patches of paint and about six inches of rubbing strake and I was receiving constant reminders that the fourteen-foot-wide locks and maybe thirty-foot-wide pounds leave very small margins for errors in boat handling.

A couple of miles above the Seend flight we tied up for the night. We were at Foxhanger Wharf, and in front of us was the bottom lock of the Caen Hill flight, one of canal-builder John Rennie's masterpieces. This lock, at the foot of the scarp slope of the Cotswolds, is numbered 22 and the Top Lock, two miles away in Devizes, is number 50. By this time you have risen about 200 feet up the hillside. *Plover* entered the bottom lock at 0910 in company with N/B *Grigory* and we tied up in Devizes nearly six hours later.

The crew of the narrowboat did all the work, provided me with cups of tea and even obliged by taking photos for the record. *Grigory* entered the locks first, *Plover* following. It took time to sort out the ropes and get the fenders the right height. I would normally secure *Plover* to the ladder halfway down the left side of the lock adjusting a short breast rope as we rose up the wall with the incoming water.

In one of the first locks, while I was adjusting fenders aft, our largest fender amidships got fouled without my noticing. When it finally freed itself the boat lurched heavily, completely pulling out about a foot of handrail round which the fender was tied. We suffered no other serious damage despite being given a pretty sharp nudge by one narrowboat. We did, however, leave odd bits of green paint at lock sides and on other long and heavy canal craft.

Several times use had to be made of the side pounds, and here *Plover*'s small size, speed and manoeuvrability came in quite useful. Each of the locks had a side pound, which in effect was a mini-reservoir in which water was temporarily stored to replace the losses due to the passage of boats up and down the flight.

By scuttling into the side pounds we helped to leave the way clear for the descending craft, which were then able to motor straight down out of one lock into the next. After that we would then follow *Grigory* up into the now empty higher lock. On the way up the flight we stopped briefly at the waterways office near the top where there was a convenient toilet and café. At Devizes Wharf I finished a lunch which I had begun at the Waterways Office. *Indaloo* arrived just before we left, and we bade farewell to the helpful *Grigory*.

We resumed cruising towards Pewsey along a lonely, often very narrow stretch with very few other craft on the move. This was the Long Pound, some fifteen miles free of locks which enabled us to make good progress for several hours, there being not only no locks but also no weed – last time I had ventured this way the miles of thick duckweed had brought the boat to a complete stop and we had had to be towed along the towpath by a couple of canoeists who had abandoned their craft! On this occasion it was the threat and finally fall of rain that stopped us, and we spent the night at Honey Street. From Honey Street the canal cuts through the Wiltshire Downs, where broad hedgeless fields sweep across the horizon and several white horses have been cut into the low chalk hills. At Wootton Rivers we started climbing again. Four locks took us up to the summit pound. At the bottom lock we shared experiences with a confident maiden lady who was piloting her 36-foot narrowboat back to Devizes after a single-handed trip to the River Thames.

I hoped in vain for a boat going my way, to reduce the effort of working the locks, but I was unlucky. In fact the short Wootton Flight was not particularly happy for us. At the second lock a 40-foot narrowboat crewed by four not very sociable men in a hurry caught up with us and my hopes of a return to the easy life soared. But this was not to be. We tailed them into the lock and following their example left the engine running rather than mess around with ropes. As the gates were opened they motored out and I put the Mariner into gear. It cut out, started again, cut out once more, ran alright in reverse but cut out again in forward gear. As the narrowboat disappeared uncharitably from view I discovered that the rope from one of our fenders was entangled round the propeller. Freeing it did not take long but it meant that I had to work the third lock on my own. Then at the fourth lock we arrived just as a broadbeam barge made its exit. As we manoeuvred to enter the chamber I had to go quite sharply into reverse, for the two dreamy ladies working the lock closed the gates in my face! When I politely brought my existence to their attention I'm sure they blushed as they apologised. Anyway they re-opened the gates for us, allowing us into the summit pound, 450 feet above sea level. The summit pound is two miles long and features the Bruce Tunnel, where the canal was dug to pass under, rather than to contour round, a hill on the edge of the Savernake forest. It is 500 yards in length, and it has no towpath but is wide enough for two narrowboats seven feet wide to ease past each other. In the old days the boats were manhandled through by men pulling on the chains suspended at intervals from the brick walls.

The descent of the canal from the summit pound towards the River Thames commences with a flurry of locks between Crofton and Great Bedwyn. At Crofton the old pumping station has been restored to working order, though with a shortened chimney. It was designed by John Rennie to pump water from a reservoir some 40 feet up to the summit pound using steam power. The two pumps are apparently the oldest working steam-powered beam engines in the world. Volunteers man the pumps for the benefit of canal enthusiasts, engineers, students of the Industrial Revolution and holidaymakers at weekends and bank holidays.

I had to work the first five locks of the Crofton flight on my own but then I got help at lock no. 60 from a group of curious bystanders who wanted to chat. Locking through is a serious business and demands total concentration, so answering questions and swapping experiences with well-meaning and often helpful strangers can be potentially dangerous. At lock 60 it almost proved to be disastrous, for *Plover* very nearly became strung up by her aft line as water flowed out of the lock. When we spotted the trouble the stern of the boat was well clear of the water and her bow was only just afloat at the end of another drum-taut length of rope. We had to partially refill the lock in a hurry in order to refloat the boat and release the lines, which were in danger of pulling out their cleats. It was a very near squeak, but no actual harm was done. I then had the help of one of the group for the next three locks, as he walked ahead with his dog to prepare each lock for us. At Great Bedwyn we called it a day and moored up above the lock before it got dark. This gave me the opportunity for a photographic stroll round the village, paying particular attention to the church and the stone museum, whose walls and yard are crowded with gravestones, some of them with whimsical epitaphs.

Working the occasional lock oneself is alright but working a succession of them, or working them for hours on end, means that progress is inevitably slow and at the expense of much hard labour, tedium and probable frustration. Effective and efficient locking is a function of team work, requiring at least two people in a team This presents the single-hander with a dilemma. If you just sit and wait for a boat going your way you may wait a very long time, during which you make absolutely no progress. On the other hand if you push on alone at least you feel that you are getting somewhere. The trouble is, of course, that just a lock or a mile behind you there may be just the boat you are looking for, one going your way!

At Great Bedwyn I decided to wait, at least for a while, rather like a predator waiting to pounce – more like a peregrine than a plover! While waiting I decided to give the boat a thorough clean-up, paying particular attention to the fenders. When I had finished she looked much better and I felt much better. But still no boat appeared.

Apart from the dirt a very noticeable defect in *Plover*'s appearance was the missing length of handrail which had pulled out in the Caen Hill flight, so I now set about repairing it. Rather to my surprise I managed to fit the damaged piece back in position with the aid of about a dozen assorted screws, making a job which was acceptable both practically and cosmetically.

It was now time for a helpful boat to appear – the whole morning had now gone – and in fact right on cue not one but two appeared. One was a narrowboat going the wrong way for me, but the second one was going my way. Unfortunately it turned out to be a huge broadbeam vessel – so big that she completely filled the 14-foot-wide locks! I had no choice but to wave her on through. It turned out that she was one of a fleet of boats operated by a charitable organisation, the Bruce's Trust, for the benefit of disabled people.

After lunch I decided to carry on without waiting any longer for help. We ought to be able to reach Hungerford at least by the end of the day. After a couple of locks we caught up with *Diana*, the broadbeam boat, which was having a lunch break. Very civilly several of the crew left their food and turned out to work *Plover* through the lock.

No two locks are exactly alike and there can be important differences in their winding gear. Those with hydraulics are smooth and easy to operate but some of those with the old rack-and-pinion gear are notoriously difficult. At two that I met during this particular afternoon the paddles of the top gates would not close properly and water continued to gush into the lock. At the first I managed to cure this by winding the paddles up again but at lock no. 70 this did not work. Eventually a level was reached and I should have been able to open the lower gates. But I couldn't – they were just stuck solid. All I could do was wait for someone to come along and help. After a while a group of cyclists came along the towpath and I flagged them down and asked for their help. They dismounted readily enough but, I sensed, with a touch of condescension and a smidgen of amusement. They put their backs confidently to the balance beams, which to their surprise, and mine, refused to yield to their combined and considerable pressure. In the end it took four of them to prise the gates reluctantly apart, and only then after a considerable amount of huffing and puffing. I think I detected a slight change in their attitude as they triumphantly picked up their machines and wearily resumed pedalling along the towpath and out of sight. I had thought they might offer to help me complete working the lock but they obviously had other things on their minds. At lock no. 73 there is an unusual arrangement with a swing bridge across the middle of the chamber This would have involved a prohibitive number of operations for a solo voyager but I was very fortunate to be helped through by a group of adults on holiday.

From the Bruce Tunnel to Hungerford the canal and the main railway line are never more than a few yards apart, and I had always wanted to take a picture of one of the Intercity trains roaring by. During my two previous transits of the canal I had always been cheated – either by an absence of trains when I was free to use the camera or because the trains rushed by when I was working a lock or avoiding another boat or some other waterside hazard. This time, after travelling several miles and missing a number of similar opportunities, I was lucky. But I was not over-pleased with the result. Of course what I should have done – and was in fact tempted to do – was to moor the boat up at one of the many places where the canal and railway are dramatically close and then patiently wait for the next train to come along. I didn't do this because we were in a hurry. Well, that's my story ...

Diana caught up with us again just a couple of locks short of Hungerford, where we spent the night. When mooring up on the towpath side at Hungerford I experienced another act of kindness. Not only had I forgotten to bring a lock handle from home but I had also left behind my two mooring stakes. Without stakes, which can be either driven into the ground like tent pegs or worked into the bank with a screwing action, one has to tie up to trees or bushes or posts or railings or whatever one can find. But of course you can't do this when moored to the towpath. It would be very bad practice and quite dangerous to have mooring lines crossing the towpath to branches or railings where walkers or cyclists could trip over them by day or by night.

After I had nosed the boat into a space behind a narrowboat I asked the skipper if I could share one of her stakes. Not only did the friendly boat owner say, 'Yes, of course', but he promptly dived below her floorboards to present me with a sturdy metal stake he carried as a spare. This was to secure the boat at the after end. That was the start of one of the many brief ad hoc friendships which one makes when cruising – either in the anchorages and marinas along the coast or along the way in the canals. This one lasted less than a day, but while it lasted it was pleasant, sincere and helpful. Once *Plover* was properly tied up, Dave Miles and his wife Mary were very helpful with information which enabled me to get the most of our overnight pit-stop. They told me I still had time to stock up with provisions at the supermarket just off the nearby High Street, and there was a rather quaint BW waterpoint not many minutes' walk away. Before turning in for the night I brought the logbook up to date, noting amongst other things that on this fine summer Saturday at the height of the holiday season we had seen only eight other boats cruising. Six of them had been going the wrong way, one had been broad beam and one had had a not very sociable crew. Hopefully things would get better tomorrow.

They did get better, lots better! When I heard Dave and Mary start their engine next morning I naturally stood by to see them off. When they told me they were going my way I asked if I could accompany them and got another, 'Of course!'

The two boats cruised together as far as Newbury, about ten miles, twelve locks and six hours farther on. This was a helping hand that I needed, and it made up for yesterday's disappointing performance. It was enjoyable too, with cups of tea and the camera passing between the boats. I am a firm believer in the law of averages, and subscribe to the view that neither good luck nor bad lasts forever, and that over time they more or less balance each other out.

Many narrowboats have strange names, and the immaculate boat belonging to Dave and Mary Miles was no exception. In fact it was unusually unusual, viz. *Four Miles On*. As I got to know them better I asked them to explain. It seemed that they, the two original Miles, had christened their boat when they had had their two young children years back. The two additions to the family meant that when they went cruising there were four members of the Miles family on board. The miles were not linear miles but people miles! When we reached Newbury we parted company with the witty couple, whose home berth was there in the marina.

At Newbury I pulled in at the wharf seeking Camping Gaz. The cylinder which I had bought at Gosport had surprised me by running out after last night's meal and I had had a cold breakfast. Alas only Calor Gas was stocked both here and farther on at an industrial estate. Still farther on at the marina the one cylinder they had turned out to be empty! This incident made me wonder about changing back to Calor Gas, which is everywhere obtainable. If not, from now on I would carry a spare cylinder on any long trip. That learning curve seems to be endless ...

From Newbury we carried on for a couple of miles to Thatcham. There were difficulties at Bulls Lock, where the swing bridge was immovable and I had to wait for help, after which we ran aground on a submerged hummock a few feet short of the mooring bollards below the lock. At Monkey Marsh I asked a young couple to help with the swing bridge and they then obligingly helped with the lock. They were unfamiliar with the canal system and the lock took an awful long time to fill. The reason was that the last user had left one of the paddles open. My helper went to attend to the problem but was unable to close the paddle – he was unaware that there was a pawl on the winding gear which had first to be released. The number of learning curves seems to be endless ...

So, well into the evening, we tied up at Thatcham at the end of the forty-ninth day of the cruise. Unable to cook on board due to lack of gas, I was happy to complete the day with a tasty chicken korma at the nearby 'Swan'.

The eighth Monday morning of our cruise was another fine sunny one, which was just as well, for there was again no hot tea or toast for breakfast. At the second lock of the day, Midgham, I exchanged experiences with a Canadian couple taking their narrowboat uphill. They told me they had a boatyard on the Pacific coast of North America but they loved the English canals and for the past eight years they have taken a summer holiday on their Nottingham-based boat. One mile farther on we were held up at a swing bridge which was operated by the simple removal of a screw bolt – which was fiendishly difficult to undo. At Woolhampton, by contrast, the swing bridge is electrically controlled, for it carries a fairly busy road. There is a locked control box, lifting barriers on the road on each side of the waterway, and a range of buttons to press in the right order – all of which takes time, probably more time than a manually operated bridge, providing you have a way with bolts.

At Aldermaston lock I got some help from a female photographer who told me she worked for *Canal Boat* magazine, and the nearby lift bridge was operated for me by a thoughtful boat owner.

At the far side of Aldermaston I walked for about a mile to a caravan site where I was able to exchange my empty Camping Gaz cylinder for a full one. Back at the canalside in the heat of the day I treated myself to an ice cream and a rest. This was a wise, thoughtful and carefully planned ruse – for along came a narrowboat passing my way! With as much dignity as feverish haste would allow I swallowed the remainder of my ice cream and cast off in the wake of *Roma*. She was a 36-footer and the recent purchase of a retired couple, Charles and Jenny. She was bound for Oxford, where they were going to gut her and give her a complete refit. They were a friendly couple, not at all in love with the Kennet and Avon and especially critical of the varied and ancient lock mechanisms. They were, therefore, in a hurry to get into the River Thames.

This was exactly the boat I had been hoping to bump into, for I too was anxious to lock out into the Thames and get back to Ipswich, where I was now overdue. When I thought about it I realised how lucky I had been to have that ice cream. If I had not bought it and had just cast off with my new gas cylinder then I would have carried on working the locks on my own until such time as *Roma* caught us up – if she ever did. Equally if I had taken just five minutes longer to walk back to the waterside with my rucksack then Charles and Jenny would have passed ahead of us without my knowing and we would again have been condemned to hard labour. Yes, that really was a lucky ice cream.

During the afternoon the two boats covered about six miles, six locks and a clutch of swing bridges. As the faster boat, *Plover* would go ahead, moor up and then prepare the next lock or bridge for *Roma*. *Plover* would then follow on and Jenny would close the gates and empty the lock. The teamwork worked well. There were problems, of course. At one lock both the lower paddles needed four pairs of hands and one swing bridge we squeezed under with millimetres to spare. At 7.30 in the evening we found moorings for ourselves at The Cunning Man on the outskirts of Reading. We agreed on an early start in the morning.

Charles and Jenny meant what they said, and it was barely half past seven when we got both boats under way. After working locks 104 and 105 we came to the County Lock in Reading. *Plover* was the lead boat, and as we approached a large road bridge and bend in the channel I had my hand on the throttle. As we passed a clump of bushes I glimpsed a notice out of the corner of my eye which said something about the lock. I reversed the boat, and indeed the notice read, 'Disembark here 50 metres to operate lock.'

The notice was on the left bank of the canal but strangely there was no pontoon, no bollards anywhere in sight, nor anything convenient at all to make fast to, just an unfriendly brick wall. Not in the mood to argue, I obediently manoeuvred *Plover* to the side, scrambled up the wall and found things out of sight to tie the boat up to. *Roma* was not yet in sight so I set off on foot to reconnoitre. On the far side of the road bridge the canal split into two arms and I saw that the lock was on the far right-hand side of the fork in the waterway. To reach it on foot would take me the best part of ten minutes so I returned to the boat intending to take her over to the lock and operate the lock from there. As I got back to the boat *Roma* appeared, and after she had gone by I cast off and followed her towards the lock gates. Then as we passed under the bridge I was amazed to see bollards for waiting craft – on the opposite side of the canal from the stupid 'Disembark here' notice and invisible from it!

Between the County Lock and Blake's Lock we slid gently through the centre of Reading, where the waterway now winds its way through the heart of a massive shopping, housing and entertainment complex where years ago was a dismal site of urban decay. A self-operated traffic-light system still operates for navigating craft. If a green light is showing you enter the system, whereupon a red light is displayed at the far end of the one-way reach, which features several sharp bends difficult for the longer 72-foot narrowboats. If a red light is shining you take your boat over to the display and press the button, which you can reach without disembarking. If the light turns green you carry on; if it doesn't you wait until a boat coming through passes out of the reach and the light turns green. A simple and effective way of avoiding collisions and also controlling traffic when flood water is discharged into the Thames.

Blake's Lock is the 105th and last one of the Kennet and Avon Canal. Just beyond lies Kennetmouth, its confluence with the River Thames. Charles and Jenny were able to lock out quickly as *Roma* already had a Thames Licence. We waved each other goodbye while the helpful lock-keeper fixed me up with a three-day visitors' licence. He explained that if I needed more time to reach Teddington, which was some fifty-odd miles downriver and is where the remit of the Environment Agency ceases, then I would be able to pay for the extra when *Plover* checked out of fresh water and back into salt.

9

Old Father Thames

The Thames is a much more relaxing waterway than the Kennet and Avon. It is about ten times the width and the locks are all electrified and manned by professional lock-keepers and there are no swing bridges. It is also beautiful, though in a very different way from the truly rural Kennet and Avon Canal. In between the widely separated towns and villages of the canal, buildings are few and unpretentious, a farm here, a pub there. By contrast, sophistication is everywhere evident on the River Thames, with many large and attractive houses lining the banks, with spacious lawns and colourful flowerbeds, willow trees and cedars, landing stages with 'Private – no mooring' notices and boat houses for shiny slipper launches or glass-fibre motor cruisers. Many of these are purported to be the properties of Arab potentates and the homes of show-biz personalities.

The manicured waterside gardens of the wealthy are matched by the immaculate and colourful displays of bedding plants at the locksides, where the lock-keepers and their spouses proudly lavish tender loving care even though there is no longer an annual competition for the best-kept lock.

Another very noticeable change I remarked was in the character of the craft using and moored along the river.

Narrowboats no longer dominated the waterway, although there were still plenty of them about. Now, however, the white, glass-fibre motor cruiser as exhibited at the Boat Show reigned supreme – forty or fifty feet long with twin diesels, bow thrusters, flying bridge and berths for six or eight. The green, eighteen foot, marine-ply sailing boat *Plover*, which had been a curiosity and an anomaly on the Kennet and Avon, remained a curiosity and an anomaly on the River Thames.

Soon after leaving Reading we passed under the traditional brickwork of Sonning Bridge and then effortlessly entered Sonning Lock, which seemed enormous.

We were now ready for some breakfast, and as both banks of the river seemed to be privately owned we ended up nosing our bows into the reeds for a half-hour break. We were now as near as we were going to get to Ascot, where my sister Phyllis and her husband Philip have a delightful cottage. I phoned them to let them know where I was and they suggested Hurley as a convenient rendezvous. Before meeting up, however, we had some serious but very enjoyable cruising to do. With the galley cleared of the breakfast breadcrumbs, we backed out of the reeds and pointed the bowsprit downstream. During a short morning we enjoyed ever-changing and never-ending interest and attraction – the wooded cliff on the loop at Wargrave, the bridge and waterfronts at historic Henley, the immaculate flowerbeds at Shiplake and Marsh locks, the manicured lawns and gardens of millionaire householders and the open country beyond Henley. When we reached Hurley the cosy charm of this part of the country was still very evident.

The lady lock-keeper at Hurley was very busy but very helpful and she found a mooring for the boat just under the footbridge. Once tied up I became feverishly busy, stuffing dirty washing into two large plastic bags and sorting out four five-litre fuel containers, disconnecting the larger of the two 12-volt batteries and trying to remember where I had stowed the trickle charger. When Phyll and Philip arrived we humped all that lot over the bridge and along to the car park through part of the lovely little village. Then I was whisked away in luxury to yet more luxury. At Peach Tree Cottage I was able to be indulgent and be indulged for a few precious, gloriously sunny hours.

While I luxuriated in a hot bath my dirty washing was detoxed, and while the ship's battery was put on charge my own batteries were given a powerful boost with a fine barbeque in the setting of a truly exquisite garden. The conversational hours flew by all too quickly, and as darkness fell I was returned to my small and simple temporary home to continue my adventure – with a topped-up battery, twenty litres of fuel, clean sweet-smelling clothes, a clean body and a well-filled tummy.

Next day it was my turn to play host in the most modest degree when my sister came aboard *Plover* for an afternoon cruise downriver. She joined the boat at Bray marina after I had spent the morning at the tiller moving the boat from Hurley down to Bray. I had enjoyed piloting *Plover* slowly past the striking, photogenic pile of Medmenham Abbey and then along the frontage of the sports-orientated abbey at Bisham and under the bridge at Marlow. There we waited twenty minutes to get through this relatively small lock. After open country around Bourne End we lazily enjoyed the woods and islets of Cliveden Reach, catching the odd glimpse of the Astor family's former hilltop residence at Cliveden, now owned by the National Trust. Then we joined the queue of craft waiting to pass through Boulter's Lock at Maidenhead.

At Bray there was another queue, but here I managed to take advantage of *Plover*'s small size by letting the lock-keeper know that although he could not see us we were in fact at the end of the queue and only 18 feet long – so maybe he could fit us into a gap among the large motor cruisers and narrowboats. He took the hint and fitted us into the very next lock, which enabled us to arrive at the Bray marina rendezvous in good time, i.e. before my sister!

The afternoon cruise commenced a trifle uncertainly. Just off the marina frontage at Bray is a sizeable island with a large building on it. – owned by Eton Rowing Club. A lady arrived with some packages and we gathered that she lived on the island and was expecting her husband to pick her up. She accepted our offer of a lift and we dropped her off at a small landing stage. As she walked off gratefully the outboard refused to start. After a number of embarrassing pulls on the starting cord I removed the engine cowling, fiddled with the throttle cable and linkage, put back the cowl and, hey presto, we were back in business. There was no further hint of trouble.

During the afternoon we cruised gently downriver past Windsor and Runnymede to Laleham, sharing a lovely sunny summer afternoon with holidaymakers on the banks of the river – some in deckchairs reading or snoozing, some in swimming costumes and some enjoying themselves in hire boats, canoes and privately owned cruisers. Philip was waiting for us at Laleham, having sorted out a very suitable pub for us for a drink and a meal. Unfortunately we took a few frustrating minutes to meet up because I had deliberately but unwisely decided to leave my mobile phone on the boat.

The following morning I was about early as usual and we were able to cast off at nine o'clock, when the lock-keepers came on duty, in continuing perfect weather. *Plover*'s three-day licence expired at midnight today but we were only five locks away from Teddington, where we would leave non-tidal waters for salt water. Before we did that there were one or two things I needed to attend to, and Thames Ditton marina, with which I was familiar, seemed to be the best place. We pulled in there after four hours' motoring.

On the way we travelled nostalgically past D'Oyly Carte Island at Weybridge, where my wife and I had a mooring back in the sixties during a nine-year period when we lived on boats on the Thames. Very soon we were drifting in reminiscent mood past Terrace Gardens, Hampton, where our boating life really began. Our introduction to boats, boating and boating people had been motivated by the shortage of funds typical of postgraduate backpackers – we had just returned from a three-year honeymoon working our passage round Europe and North Africa. We had paid £60 for the unfinished conversion of a 20-foot bailey bridge pontoon and then lived happily in our *Nutshell* for three and a half years, during which we just about completed the conversion. The work took so long because we were having such a marvellous time! The boating life suited us very well until births and deaths in the family made landlubbers of us again. At Molesey we passed through the largest lock on the Upper Thames and then drifted under Hampton Court bridge and past the palace.

At Thames Ditton marina I bought some odds and ends and a length of hosepipe for the portable bilge pump but still failed to get it working. We continued on past Kingston to Teddington with the river virtually our own. Rain threatened and began to fall as we approached Richmond Bridge, which we passed under before tying up for the night to a derelict old hulk in a strong running tide. Not long after I had finished adjusting ropes and fenders a youngish couple of lads came along in a skiff and reprimanded me for mooring up without permission. 'You should have asked!' they complained, though 'asked who?' remained a mystery, there being no notice on the boat and no markings on the buoys.

Friday 12 August, the Glorious Twelfth, was in fact anything but glorious. For a change it was grey, cool, overcast and windy, with much rubbish floating about. Slack water was at 0810 and that was when we cast off. During the next hour we motored past the London Apprentice at Isleworth and Syon Park, Twickenham, both on the Middlesex bank, with Kew Gardens not very noticeable on the opposite Surrey bank

At Kew the tideway opens out and we soon passed the finishing post of the university boat race at Mortlake. The tide was now ebbing fast and helped us on our way as more and more mud became exposed. The bridges across the river now came in irregular succession. No two were alike, and the most interesting were those at Wandsworth, Hammersmith and Chelsea plus, of course, the Albert suspension bridge. We navigated virtually alone all the way to the Tate Gallery, seeing just one rower, one rigid inflatable and one motor cruiser heading upstream.

As we thrilled past the sights of London I relied upon the autopilot to enable me to take digital images. Between Lambeth and Tower Bridge I was particularly trigger-happy but I had to be careful for the tide was running strongly and of course there were many fast-ferry and day-trip boats whizzing about amongst the driftwood and the rafts of moored lighters. To my horror the camera batteries failed as we were approaching London Bridge. By throttling back a little I managed to change them in a few hairy minutes as we shot under the bridge and avoided other navigating craft, huge commercial mooring buoys and rafted-up barges.

After Tower Bridge the high drama flattens out, and in any case the mind has to be concentrated upon getting safely out of the river and into the safe haven of the Limehouse Basin. This is situated on the north bank of the river about a couple of miles below Tower Bridge. The entrance is narrow, obscure and at right angles to the course of the river. Just inside the entrance is a ridiculously small waiting pontoon and, immediately beyond that, two large lock gates.

I had no difficulty locating the entrance, as my little boat is no stranger to Limehouse. But this was the first time that I had approached it from upstream. Crabbing *Plover* across the river and into a position sufficiently upstream of the entrance to allow for the vicious ebb tide required a certain amount of care and a fair amount of throttle, but once out of the tide it was necessary to throttle back quickly and edge over to the pontoon ready to hop ashore with ropes at the ready.

Once tied up one has no means of getting off the pontoon to make contact with the lock-keeper. There is now a CCTV camera focused on the pontoon, however, and all one can do is hope that the camera is working and that someone is on duty. We were lucky. A lock-keeper soon appeared, confirmed that we did want to lock through, and warned us to keep well clear of the gates until they were fully open. A while later, after the discharge of a considerable volume or water, my little boat was able to motor into and then out of the lock and into the familiar tranquillity of the Limehouse Basin.

10

The last leg

We made fast to the public moorings inside the basin and just a boat length or two from the headquarters of the Cruising Association. I was delighted and relieved for several reasons. The inland waterways leg of the safari was now over and this left only one remaining leg to complete – the passage down the Thames and round the Essex coast back to the River Orwell. Barring some late misfortune, mistake or accident it looked as though *Plover* and I were going to bring off an unlikely success. And most importantly, I was going to be back home three weeks before the planned joint celebration of Margot and myself tottering into the eighties. Lastly, the need to travel home for the anniversary, returning to the boat a week or so later to complete the final leg, was going to be obviated – one bite of this pomegranate-sized cherry was going to be enough.

With these thoughts running through my mind I had some lunch and then set about converting *Plover* from inland-waterways mode back to coastal-cruising mode. This took the rest of the day. First of all the mast had to be unlashed and then the standing rigging sorted out. That done, by agreement with the lock-keeper, I took the boat over to the marina pontoons to get the mast re-stepped.

For this job I needed the help of two able-bodied males. The father and son off a nearby large seagoing cruiser happily obliged, and I was chuffed when the whole operation went without a hitch or a glitch. Back on the public moorings, I could now attach the boom, attend to the running rigging and bend on the roller-reefing genoa and the mainsail.

I had one important job left – to top up the fuel tanks. After dipping the tanks I found that there was less than thirty litres on board. Under normal conditions that ought to be ample to get us back home, even if we motored the whole way unaided by sail. But it would not leave much of a margin for changes of plan, emergencies, etc. So I unfolded my little trolley, strapped on three containers and set off along the towpath of the River Lee for the Commercial Road in nearby Brixton. I had remembered that there was a filling station quite near which I had used on previous visits. To my dismay I now found that it had closed down. Nobody could tell me where the nearest one now was but it was obviously not at all near. Disappointed and annoyed, I returned to the boat resolved to take a chance. All I had to do now was book my exit from the basin with the lock-keeper and we were ready for the final leg.

Well satisfied with the day, I had a shower over in the lockside facility, returned to the boat to eat, and then went over to the Cruising Association to relax over a drink in the bar. After a few minutes on my own the crew of the cruiser who had helped me get the mast up came into the bar and seemed pleased to sit down for a chat and to swap experiences, thus ending the day on a very pleasant note.

The early-morning forecast was not encouraging – southerly or southwesterly winds force 4/5 occasionally 6 for inland waters! These circumstances ruled out any thoughts of bashing my way home during the day, which would have been quite feasible given fair weather. The most I could hope for was to make the best possible haste downriver, and scuttle into Hole Haven or Leigh Creek when the tide turned foul. When the winds died down I could then finish the job.

When we locked out into the Thames the ebb tide had already been running for an hour so we could count on its assistance for about another five hours. Out in the river, conditions were calm under a grey sky and we began to make good speed under power.

Although the tidal Thames below Tower Bridge cannot compare with the rich tapestry of Westminster and the City there is still a great deal of maritime, architectural and historical interest, though it is less condensed. Forty to fifty years ago, when London was still a major and very busy port, enclosed docks festooned both banks of the river and ocean-going ships from all over the world and their tugs congested the channel and the wharves. The general aspect of the river was grimy, industrial and a dirty grey with the water a dangerous broth of broken barrels, baulks of timber, parts of boats, dead dogs and much, much more. Nowadays shipping above Tilbury is insignificant but the riversides have been and are continuing to be upgraded, and the water quality has improved to such an extent that occasional live seals – and in January 2006 a bottle-nosed whale – now forage where dead cats and other carcases used to predominate. So it was that we started off with the camera focused on the classical waterfront at Greenwich, the observatory and the *Cutty Sark*. We took note of the continuing developments around Canary Wharf, where the annual Boat Show is now held, and the deserted and ill-fated but still elegant Millennium Dome.

After sweeping through the correct gate of the Thames Barrier at Woolwich, as directed by the large green illuminated arrows, we slowed down shortly afterwards to give way to the bustling vessels of the Woolwich free ferry. A rather dull stretch comes next, embellished only by a couple of wind turbines. Their rotating blades indicated that there must be enough wind for sailing, so at Erith I unfurled the genoa and we sped along in fine style. As we glided under the Queen Elizabeth Bridge at Dartford I contrasted our lonely, peaceful, steady but admittedly pedestrian progress with that of the ceaseless impatient traffic up above on the M25.

Next came the Tilbury and Gravesend area, where ships, tugs and pilot boats create interest and call for due attention and a proper deference to those who work on the water. Between Tilbury and Southend the widening estuary, with its occasional shipping and oil refineries, dominates the scene. With the jib still unfurled we then motor-sailed all the way to Holehaven in fine style. The 35-mile trip down the Thames had occupied a well-spent morning.

Around noon, as we approached the West Blyth buoy, we had a bit of a scare when we touched bottom on the mud flats off the Kent shoreline, but after a few bumps and some lively evasive action we found our way back into deep water. The tide was now running against us and, bearing in mind the unfavourable forecast, we sought shelter in Holehaven. The entrance to this creek is not easy to find at low water neaps and to start with we anchored off. While waiting for more water the unforeseen but heavy wash from a tanker way out in the buoyed channel surged over our shallow anchorage and unshipped the rudder, which floated away before I could reach it with the fully extended boathook. I just had to recover the rudder so I watched its course, which fortunately was into and not out of the creek, and pinpointed its probable grounding site. I then got the inflatable out of its locker and commenced inflating it in the cockpit. This took about ten minutes in all but, as I prepared to launch it over the side, the skipper of a nearby boat rowed over brandishing our rudder. He explained that he had seen me furiously pumping up the Avon and had wondered why on earth I was doing so; then he had spotted the rudder floating towards him and had put two and two together.

With the wind rising and the forecast rain threatening, I decided to move into the creek proper. I had been hoping to motor the six miles further down the estuary to Leigh Creek later in the day but clearly it was unlikely that we would make any more ground this day. Alas I now found that the anchor was fouled and I could not haul it up. After a period of anxious exercises I eventually managed to free it by motoring forward – to my great relief. I was beginning to fall out of love with Holehaven. The creek is the home of numbers of commercial fishing boats and there were no vacant moorings so we had to anchor again, rather anxiously.

With rain forecast and in the air I rigged up the lightweight boom cover in rather gusty conditions. One extra-strong gust carried away the plastic forward hatch cover, which I have to rig to keep out heavy rain and spray because the hatch leaks. With the tide flooding rapidly into the creek, and the wind rising, it was difficult to be sure what was happening to our anchor. We were certainly swinging closer and closer to a small open fishing boat on the nearest mooring. Before turning in I got a line through his buoy so that we would be safe if our anchor dragged during the night. Actually the night passed without incident but at 0600 we got a nudge from the dayboat so I eased myself out of my sleeping bag and adjusted our lines and fenders. I noticed that we had a rope round the prop again so I cut that free with the kitchen knife, working from the inflatable. I also noticed that one of the two powerful springs of the outboard bracket was broken – this no doubt explained why the motor was bouncing about so erratically off Boscastle. With no prospect of getting away today (winds force 6–7 'for a time' were forecast), I did a thorough check on the rear section of the boat – the Mariner, the bracket, the rudder and Tillerpilot. I rewired the autopilot but it still didn't work, even though both batteries tested green.

I spent virtually the whole day doing odd jobs around the boat, inside and out but also dealing with recurrent mooring crises. These were due, in large measure, to the veritable hooley which was blowing and raising a minor chop even here in this protected creek. Around midday at low water I decided, after some dithering, to get away from the day launch, which we were uncomfortably close to all the time. I hauled up the anchor and we crossed the channel and dropped the hook in deep water close to the steeply rising mud bank.

As the tide flooded in, the mud became covered and the whole geography of the creek changed out of all recognition. After a period of careful observation, and after veering more chain, I became convinced that we were not safe and were showing signs of dragging. Come high water we almost certainly would. With this wind blowing there was little likelihood of boats moving so I decided to pick up a mooring. I selected one that looked little used and after three attempts managed to defeat the strong tide and wind and get a line to it. We had to be content tied up unconventionally, stern first. This turned out to be a blessing, for I soon discovered why the mooring appeared little used. There were two buoys, one large, the other the size of a small football. There was no way of getting a line round the large one so I put two lines round the smaller one. With wavelets lapping the hull and the wind howling in the rigging I was sipping a cup of tea in the cabin when I realised that we were adrift and towing the small float! In the nick of time I managed to get the outboard started and steer *Plover* away from the perilously near sea wall and other moored craft.

By now I was thoroughly disenchanted with Holehaven, which I preferred to call Hellhaven, and I wondered if I would ever find a safe mooring in this muddy, windblown, tide-riven, grey, nasty, neglected, unfriendly and dangerous hole. By motoring well up the creek I did, in the end, find what looked like a safe mooring, whose buoy had a top ring, and there we managed to survive until the following day.

The teatime shipping forecast for the Thames area was for north or northwest winds force 5–6 decreasing 3–4 – conditions I could possibly cope with. I deflated the Avon Redstart and stowed it on board and generally made ready for departure in the morning. After dark a beautiful half-moon suggested that the weather was changing for the better, and this was confirmed at 0535 when the wind force predicted was reduced to 4–5 becoming variable 3 or less.

We cast off from Holehaven at 0810 after tying the football-sized buoy to the mooring we were vacating. Once out of the creek and into the Thames I unfurled the jib to help us on our way. There was a little wind from the northwest, the sea was calm, there was a lot of cloud, and it was quite cool.

After an hour we were off Southend pier and we began the rounding of the Maplin Sands. We avoided the wreck of the *Phoenix* and the long obstruction off Shoebury, and by 1100 we had reached the western Blacktail Spit. There are firing ranges on Foulness Island, and as we headed for the Swin channel some heavy artillery started firing with deep-throated crunches – and to my amazement I actually saw, for the first time ever, the plume of water where a shell landed quite a distance ahead of us! The firing only lasted a few minutes and was obviously not very accurate so I didn't bother to fire back.

By midday we were approaching the Whitaker Beacon in warm, misty conditions with little wind but a helpful ebb tide. I calculated that we could be home in not much more than four hours and phoned a message to that effect through to Margot. That was an over-optimistic calculation and an ill-judged communication, for ten minutes later we were hard aground on the Whitaker Sand with a revised ETA of some time tomorrow.

I cursed myself for casual navigation, the more reprehensible on a falling tide with no echo sounder. We lost three valuable hours sitting on our bilge keels, but those three hours meant that when we refloated we had lost the tide. Instead of breezing along happily to the entrance to Harwich Harbour and then being helped up the Orwell on the young flood we now had to punch the tide all the way across the Blackwater estuary over to Clacton and then up the coast to the Naze, which we reached at 2000 instead of 1400. The only consolation for this stupid error was that by the time we refloated the wind had freshened and we were able to motor-sail, with all canvas set, all the way to the Naze with the main beautifully filled, the genoa drawing nicely and the boat heeled 15 degrees – as much as I could handle at times. This was by far the best sailing of the whole trip.

The sun was setting as we rounded the Naze. I had decided to overnight in the Walton Backwaters and as we now headed into the wind I furled the jib. Our progress over the ground using only the motor against the tide became painfully slow, and in the failing light I was anxious to pick up the small and unlit channel buoys marking the channel to the Backwaters before dark

As we crossed the Pye Sand we were lucky to spot a yacht on our bows heading up the channel for Stone Point. With a burst of throttle wide open we tucked in behind her until safely inside, where I got the mainsail down. When I dipped the fuel tanks I found that there were still twelve litres on board. Yesterday we used eight litres punching the tide from Foulness to Stone Point, and I calculated that we were using a litre every forty minutes and covering four nautical miles per hour.

After anchoring I scribbled a brief note in the deck log: 'Before eating, a reflective glass of wine with a misty moon tracking towards *Plover*. My last night on boat – relieved, pleased, amazed, chuffed and encouraged. Too old! Past it – I don't think so! Home tomorrow.'

Early morning there was thick fog, which rapidly cleared to reveal a perfect summer day. I spent the last morning of the cruise sprucing up the boat and organising my return. I inflated the Redstart, which I used for a photo shoot and to row ashore to explore Stone Point a little, something I had never done before. By a strange chance I was hailed by the yacht club member from whom I had bought the inflatable five or more years ago. He was rowing ashore with his children.

At 1330 I thought to set off on the last few miles of our cruise by sailing off – but I should have known better. As soon as the anchor broke out of the mud the wind had us in the bank before I could scramble back to the cockpit. Unpleased, I had to get the sails down again, start the motor and reverse off. With the sails re-set we caught the early flood off the North Shelf and then had a fast passage up river. I saw more yachts in Pennyhole Bay, Harwich Harbour and the Orwell than I had seen anywhere since leaving Portsmouth. Off Roman Path a dredger did a U-turn right in front of us but I was in no mood to argue. Finally we passed under the Orwell Bridge and I got the sails down. When the little boat, which I had considered selling or scrapping at Newport, Isle of Wight, but which I now loyally respected, was shipshape and Bristol fashion, we motored back to the OYC pontoon to be greeted by an

Evening Star photographer, who took scores of photos. Our cruise was over!

But the memories linger on and almost all of them are happy ones. In two crowded months I had hopped from buoy to buoy and headland to headland round the interesting ports and beautiful coasts of southern England, returning through green and pleasant inland waterways. I had witnessed a memorable and spectacular maritime commemoration. The weather had mostly been very good and we had survived a sample of the not so good. Everywhere I had met with kindness and goodwill; I had made some good friends. I had learned a lot – about the boat, about boating and, unfortunately, about myself. Most satisfying of all, I had got my sea legs firmly back under the cabin table.

Statistics

(mostly approximate)

Dates of cruise	19 June – 16 Aug 2005
Length of cruise	58 days
Lost due to weather	13 days
Otherwise in port	6 days
Distance logged	1200 statute miles

Hours on passage

purely under sail	21
motor-sailing	56
motoring – canals, rivers	77
motoring – coastal	128
Total	282

Costs incurred

240 litres petrol & oil	£215
Harbour dues, licences	£150
Boat repairs, charts, etc	£228
Food & drink	£210
Miscellaneous	£100
Total	£903

The Seatrekkers

The Seatrekker was an estuary cruiser designed by C R Holman of West Mersea, Essex. It would appear that the design was commissioned by Wrights of Ipswich, who retained sole rights of production. Seemingly very few were in fact constructed. There were several versions on offer. A stub-keel version concealing a centreplate was an alternative to twin keels. An inboard Stuart Turner engine could be installed, and in the cockpit rolled decks were an option. All the boats were constructed of marine ply.

It is surprising that the class had so little success – it was ideal for exploring the sands and muds of the east-coast estuaries and swatchways and performed well under sail. Of the half dozen or so built I owned three at one time. The first was *Virgo*, a smart little centreboarder bought from a fellow Orwell Yacht Club member. She came to grief in the 'hurricane' of October 1987 when chocked up in a local boatyard. A much larger craft fell onto her and she was a total constructive loss.

During the ensuing winter I found two other Seatrekkers in local yards and I bought them both. The first was *Plover*, then a sorry, neglected shambles with bilge keels and a dubious inboard Vire 6 engine and a forward hatch. The second was *Mike Crow*, which had been possessed in lieu of mooring fees. With three boats but only two masts (*Virgo*'s had been snapped in two), I embarked upon an extensive programme of cannibalisation, taking advantage of the plethora of second-hand gear on the market. I hesitantly stepped a grossly oversized mast on *Plover*, from which I eventually lopped off the top three feet.

Eventually I finished up with three serviceable craft, two of which I sold to friends. My bilge-keel version proved to be something of a carthorse compared to the centreplate *Virgo* version and in the end I fitted a bowsprit in an attempt to reduce excessive weather helm. The Vire 6-horsepower engine proved to be a nightmare and I scrapped it for a Stuart Turner – and when that predictably worked itself to death I was persuaded to try a well-spoken-of Vire 7. That powerful little motor served intermittently well for several years until finally prohibitive repair estimates forced me to abandon inboard engines for outboards.

Virgo and *Mike Crow* are no more – possibly leaving *Plover* the last of the Seatrekkers.

Paul Packwood

Paul Packwood was born in 1924 in Bristol but considers himself an Ipswichian. A very average scholar, his most vivid memories of his youth are of low-flying Heinkels, Junkers and doodlebugs, long solo exploratory cycle rides through the Suffolk countryside and wartime school forestry camps. These inspired him towards a career in forestry, with ambitions focused on British Columbia.

Military service from 1944 to 1948 changed all that, however, and demobilisation saw him taking a degree in economics, with journalism and politics in mind. He also became very mindful of another ex-service student, who rapidly became his wife. In 1950 they set off on a three-year honeymoon, backpacking their way across Europe from the North Cape to Gibraltar and then crossing the strait to North Africa.

Aged nearly 30 and without a decent CV, nine months' unemployment was eventually ended with two years in the Dagenham youth service, followed by nine years teaching in Wimbledon. During this time he and his wife were living on various boats on the River Thames. Two of their three children were born at this time.

The death of his father coinciding with the wrecking of the Cornish yawl which was then his home saw him return to Ipswich, where he enjoyed working as the founder and leader of the Murrayside Club – a youth club with many differences.

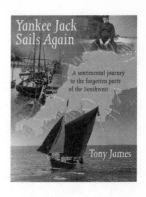
YANKEE JACK SAILS AGAIN
A sentimental journey to the forgotten ports of the Southwest
TONY JAMES

John Short, better known as shanty-man 'Yankee Jack', knew
the ports of the Southwest Peninsula over a hundred years
ago, when they were all busy commercial harbours. Tony
James revisits the ports, sailing into them in a 19-foot open
boat – a replica of a Bristol Channel flatner he built himself.
He rediscovers a forgotten world peopled by characters who,
a century on, are still larger than life.

Women and children fighting invaders with sticks and stones, 20 million pilchards caught
within 24 hours, cargoes as diverse as soap, raisins and bullocks' horns – the Southwest's
colourful maritime past has been brought to life in this evocative new book.

Beautifully written and wryly observed, *Yankee Jack Sails Again* is a unique and enthralling
voyage of discovery – an absorbing, remarkable book.

Illustrated with over 230 stunning photographs, many previously unpublished, spanning 150 years of
maritime history • ISBN 0-9550243-2-3 • £14.95

UP THE CREEK
A lifetime spent trying to be a sailor
TONY JAMES

Up the Creek charts Tony James's unintentional voyage from his
father's broad bean bed, in landlocked Derbyshire, to a marina
in Somerset via the Caribbean, the Persian Gulf and the bottom
of a swimming pool in Ottery St Mary. On the way Tony gathers
a motley crew of unfogettable eccentrics and maritime misfits,
brought to hilarious life by his acute observation of the ridiculous
and by his wry acceptance that, whatever happens at sea, things
can only get worse. The funniest and most original sailing book
for years.

**'Laugh-out-loud funny ... unlike any other sailing
memoir ... destined to become a classic'**
>   *STEPHEN SWANN* – Editor,
>   *Traditional Boats and Tall Ships*

With a foreword by Stephen Swann • Illustrated
ISBN 0-9547062-7-7 • £9.95

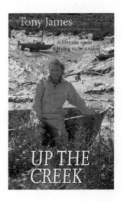

JOSEPH CONRAD: MASTER MARINER

PETER VILLIERS

Before he published his first novel in 1895, Joseph Conrad spent 20 years in the merchant navy, eventually obtaining his master's ticket and commanding the barque *Otago*. This book, superbly illustrated with paintings by

Mark Myers, traces his sea-career and shows how Konrad Korzeniowski, master mariner, became Joseph Conrad, master novelist. Alan Villiers, world-renowned author and master mariner under sail, was uniquely qualified to comment on Conrad's life at sea, and the study he began has been completed by his son, Peter Villiers.

'A book that finally does justice to Conrad's time at sea'
Traditional Boats and Tall Ships

Illustrated with 12 paintings in full colour by Mark Myers RSMA F/ASMA

ISBN 0-9547062-9-3 • £14.95

CRUISE OF THE CONRAD

A Journal of a Voyage round the World, undertaken and carried out in the Ship JOSEPH CONRAD, 212 Tons, in the Years 1934, 1935, and 1936 by way of Good Hope, the South Seas, the East Indies, and Cape Horn

ALAN VILLIERS

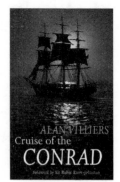

In 1934 the Australian sailor and writer Alan Villiers set out to fulfil his life's ambition – to obtain, equip and sail a full-rigged ship around the world, and enthuse others with his own love of sail before the opportunity was lost for ever. He was successful. His record of that extraordinary journey, more odyssey than voyage, was first published in 1937. In this new edition, complete with a short biography of Alan Villiers and richly illustrated with his own photographs, it will inspire a new generation of sailors and sea-enthusiasts.

'No other book like this will ever be written'
The Sunday Times

With a foreword by Sir Robin Knox-Johnston • Illustrated with photographs
ISBN 0-9547062-8-5 • £12.95

MUDLARK'S GHOSTS
And the restoration of a Herreshoff Meadow Lark

IAN SCOTT

Mudlark, built in 1953, is a modified version of the iconic Meadow Lark, a shallow-draft leeboard sharpie ketch designed by L Francis Herreshoff. But she is about to sink. Ian Scott decides to save her, and to do the work himself. This is the story of why and how he devoted many years to the restoration, and of what he learned in the process – about wooden boats, the timbers they are made of, the designers and craftsmen who make and repair them, the tools they use and, not least, about himself.

'Most how-I-restored-an-old-wooden-boat books will make your eyes bleed. Not this one. Ian Scott's *Mudlark's Ghosts* is literate, intelligent, and informative – an inspiration'
> PETER H SPECTRE – Editor, *The Mariner's Book of Days*

'Into this world of mass production comes a one-off book by a one-off author about a one-off boat ... required reading for anyone contemplating doing up an old wooden boat'
> PETE GREENFIELD

Illustrated • ISBN 0-9550243-1-5 • £14.95

THE LONE RANGER STORY
From salvage tug to super yacht

JOHN JULIAN

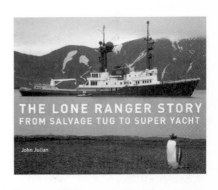

Lone Ranger worked as a salvage tug (then named *Simson*) and towed some of the largest oil installations ever built during twenty of the most challenging years in the history of the business. During the mid-1990s she embarked on a second career and has become the world's pre-eminent exploration yacht. As befits her name she goes to the cold extremes of latitude where few other ships are found, but is also seen in the warm seas of the Caribbean and Mediterranean. Here, her proud and purposeful lines stand out among pleasure craft that have never battled through a storm to take a distressed ship in tow or stood by a bulk carrier threatened with destruction on a lee shore. She begins her fourth decade as supremely seaworthy as ever with more long voyages in prospect, thanks to the vision and commitment of her owner and crew.

ISBN 0-9550243-0-7 • £19.95